THE TWO SONS OF GOD

The Son Of Man and The Son Of God

What The Bible "Really" Says

Charles S. Brown

THE TWO SONS OF GOD

The Son Of Man and The Son Of God

What The Bible Really Says

Charles S. Brown

http://www.crystalbooks.org

This Edition published in **New Zealand** by **Crystal Publishing**.
P.O. Box 60042, Titirangi, West Auckland, **NEW ZEALAND**.

First Edition 2005
Second Edition 2007

Final Edition 2012

ISBN 978-0-9582813-9-3

Contents

Acknowledgements

Crystal Publishing gratefully and singularly acknowledges **Ferrar Fenton** – long deceased from the physical world – yet whose monumental work of re-translating **The Bible** finally permitted certain key questions in centuries-old conflicts between science and religion – specifically Creation versus Evolution – to be perfectly reconciled. Through his intuitively-correct translation of **The Book of Genesis**, particularly Chapters 1 and 2, he has singularly rendered *every other* "Genesis" translation – that does not accord with his correct, and thus powerfully-guided, insights – irrelevant. Near-future events will unequivocally bear out the truth of this statement.

His crucial *spiritual* insights have therein returned to **The Creator** that which is **His** – **the Majesty and Power of The Pure Truth of His stupendous and humanly-incomprehensible Creation**. Fenton has therewith bequeathed to the worlds of science and religion the ordained foundation upon which to build, within their Disciplines:

The 'Harmonising Truth' about Creation and Evolution; and thus the True Origins of Man!

Precisely *because* Fenton has *correctly understood* the ***Creation/Evolution*** reality deriving from **Immutable Divine Law**, the logical extrapolation from such sure insight also logically means that his translation and insights thus offer greater enlightenment than do other mainstream Bibles.

In the context of the subject matter of this Booklet, Fenton's correct translation of **The Book of Genesis** therefore permits certain questions about the **Life, Death and Resurrection of Jesus** to be answered more logically than is possible with other Bibles. More especially on the key aspect of Jesus's birth, since **The Son Of God Himself** – in order for a time to be a "man among men" – had also to be born of a woman of earth.

With specific regard to the contentious notion of **The Two Sons Of God**, Fenton's especial insight there, too, offers a particularly revealing dimension into this *unequivocal reality*.

So among the very many Bible translations inundating global Christendom, **Ferrar Fenton's Bible** stands as the strongest overall.

Introduction

The *especial* purpose of this Booklet — the subject matter of which is very substantially derived from its Parent Publication:

BIBLE "MYSTERIES" EXPLAINED:
[Revised Second Edition]
Understanding "Global Societal Collapse" from The "Science" in The Bible;
What Every Scientist, Bible Scholar and Ordinary Man Needs to Know! —

— is to bring to the attention of the Christian Church, particularly, but global humanity as a whole, *including the world of science*, the knowledge of:

"The Two Sons of God!"

Given the so-long-held belief of global Christendom awaiting the ostensible return of **Jesus** as the *only* **Son of God**, such a notion as **Two Sons** would surely be dismissed, unfortunately very wrongly – *as near-future events will prove* – as arrant nonsense. So two thousand million odd Christians stand *completely oblivious* to this quite stupendous reality. And the rest of global humanity...? Well: In their myriad religions, sects,

7

dogmas, doctrines and cults; would probably not be the least bit interested. There, however, in that very erroneous notion, the vast majority who would so reject would err terribly.

For the knowledge of **The Two Sons** [**Son** meaning *Part* or *Extension*] of **The Creator** of *all* men is clearly revealed in <u>both</u> **The Bible** <u>and</u> **The Book of Esdras** in **The Apocrypha**. From these primary Works of Truth we will extract the very information that will reveal, elucidate and proclaim, the most *Crucial Imperative* for *every* human being on earth *at this present time*.

In the very first instance, the question of '**a**' Son of God incarnating on earth obviously presupposes a precise mechanism for such an entry into the world of we humans. Was it, is it, the same process that virtually all earth-creatures must undergo? For 'down here', a physical/material body is imperative. Or is there a different process for a **'Son'** of **The Creator** – as Christianity in particular would opine?

If we briefly note the ongoing contention of Creation versus Evolution, then on this *exact* subject a key question has very serious resonance for all 'men on earth' – thus also a **Son of God** here for a time as "a man among men". Currently, one branch of earth-science is single-mindedly striving to "prove" that the 'human genome' reigns supreme as "the life-force of earthman". So, it is *either* the "genomic" aspect of we, a complete entity – that though ostensibly the 'life-force' for earth-science nonetheless rots away with the physical body at death – *or* an animating force *separate from* the physical body. So, only one or the other, not both.

If – as *we* unequivocally accept – it *is* 'the separable animating force', then **Who** or **What** is *responsible* for it? In other words, **Who** or **What** gave us, indeed *permitted* us, *conscious life*? Empirical earth-science would tend *towards* the **what**. Most religions, however, would probably *state* the **Who**!

In 2009 the History Channel sought a definitive answer to this "apparent" quandary in questions such as:
"Where did [this] life come from? What IS life, exactly?" And:
"Is it chemical, spiritual, <u>or a combination of both?</u>"

And perhaps more crucially here – the National Geographic Channel asks:
"How did *non-living* material <u>*come to life*</u>?"

(Emphases mine.)

Should we regard these questions as scientific or religious – or both? As is the nature of the beast, there cannot possibly be two very different answers in diametric opposition to each other here. It is either one thing or the other. For the very many who obviously *are* interested enough to want to know, the issue is not at all clear-cut. We, of course, by simple and logical analyses of *both sides* of this really *unnecessary* debate, have already made our unequivocal determination.

So: What forces or processes *did* bring or *give life* to *inanimate* matter? Since we do not at all accept the completely illogical idea that *inanimate matter* can – *out of itself* – actually provide the *animating mechanism* to *somehow give life to* inanimate matter, the only alternative that must necessarily be valid here is the existence of a *non-material* life-force to *so animate*. That being the most logical scenario; what form and/or process might facilitate such an amazing outcome? Paradoxically, *perhaps even perversely*, an outcome which permits us the reasoning intelligence to not only debate just the yes or no of our very *reason for being*, but every other question that naturally arises from that reality?

The purpose of this Introduction is not so much to explain the Creation-process in any great depth – for we have already done so in the Parent Work i.e., Chapter 2: **The Origins of Man: Genesis and Science Agree!** – but to especially *elucidate* the *key point* that provides the *definitive answer*

9

to the **Who** of Creation's *life-force reality.* Even though the whole of the Parent Work states it clearly, this question of **The Two Sons [Parts] Of God** being the most **Crucial Imperative** for *all* of global humanity in *all* its diverse cultures, religions and scientific paradigms, means that an elucidatory explanation of **"The Two"** is naturally paramount in this analysis.

To that end, *and for **both** science and **all** religions in this case,* we will briefly notate explanatory Scripture from The Book of Genesis. Precisely because The Bible *is* a book of **Foundational-science**, it really does reveal the processes *whereby* the animating life-force we all must necessarily possess in order to live is *gifted* to us. Inherent within that especial Work, therefore, is the *very clear* **Revelation of The Two.** And, moreover, *which* of **The Two** is **"The Who"** of the life-force for Creation. Reproduced more or less verbatim from Chapter 2 of the Parent Work, the following Scriptures from Chapters 1 and 2 of "Genesis" *clarify the fact.* From the Jerusalem Bible:

> "Now the earth was a formless void. There was darkness over the deep, and God's *spirit* hovered over the water."

> "But the Earth was unorganised and empty; and darkness covered its convulsed surface; while the *breath* of GOD rocked the surface of its waters."

> (The Holy Bible in Modern English.
> Ferrar Fenton.)

The unequivocal reference to a **"Creative Spirit"** clearly shows that it was not God Himself Who Created the "heavens and the earth", but **He Who was with Him!** The very fact that it is so written reveals that the ancient writers of the original texts *understood this clearly.* We should readily understand, however, that Creation itself proceeded only *according* to **God's Plan**, under *His Power and Authority,*

but *through He* Who was *with* **God** as a *Part* of **Him**.
The Christian Church teaches that Jesus is the only Son
[Part] of God. And that, therefore, the Creative Spirit must
be Him. The following Scripture from John 1:1-3 can certainly be *interpreted* that way. [Emphases mine.]

> "The **WORD** existed **in the beginning**, and the
> **WORD** was *with* God and the **WORD** *was* God.
> *He* was present *with* God at the beginning.
> **All** came into existence by means of *Him*; and noth-
> ing came into existence apart from *Him*."

So we immediately see that *at the time when Creation
came into being*, there was not just **God** and the empty
void. There was **Another** – *with* God! The key question
here is:

Who was *"He Who was present with God...?"* Was 'He'
Jesus, as is perhaps currently accepted? Or was 'He' the
Other, to **Whom** we refer?

The key point here once more is that **Whomever** was
present **with** God was there **at the beginning** [i.e.; *when
Creation came into being*]. That is what must be seriously grasped from the Scripture. Moreover, the use of the
personal pronoun **He** is a clear pointer as to *Who this particular One actually is*. As a second vital pointer to the answer, the Scripture also clearly states that; *"...the Word
that was with God..."* was the *"...He Who was present
at the beginning."* And that; *"...all came into existence
by means of Him!"*
To reiterate the key point of that particular Scripture again:

He Who was **with** God was **also** the **Word of** God too,
and that **all** came into existence by means of **Him**! A mystery perhaps? No! Not a mystery at all because The Bible
identifies **Who** that **"Other"** actually **Is**. Further on in this
Booklet, we will *revisit* these exact points and, from **The
Book of Revelation**, reveal and extend, *for science and*

religion, the knowledge of **"Who"** of **The Two Sons Of God** was *with God* 'at the beginning'.

For 'genome scientists' once more, an insight into the 'two parts to man'. From Job 10:9-12, Fenton. [Emphases mine.]

> "Remember You made me from clay,
> That to dust You will make me return!
> And did You not curdle the milk,
> And fixed me together like cheese,
> Then clothed me with skin, and with flesh,
> And with bones and with muscles compact?
> And gave me my life and my reason,
> Then *last*, **fixed my Spirit in me**?"

And from Chapter 1 of the Parent Work:

Crucial Imperative No 2:

> That we, the human beings of planet Earth, are not solely a physical entity, but also necessarily possess a *non-material* inner animating core: *For the physical* **cannot** *– and therefore* **does not** *– animate the physical!*

The knowledge of "The Two Sons Of God" *could perhaps* be designated as the greatest "Bible Mystery" of all. Not because it *is* a mystery, but because the Christian world, comprising close to one third of humanity, is completely *unaware* of this crucially important fact — or would probably refuse to believe it. For global Christendom, therefore, such a "blasphemous idea" would surely occupy the *not possible* category. Unfortunately, however, that denial *will bring* the severest "reaping" of all. Notwithstanding the too-long-held and appalling 'Christian-church distortion' of the 'sacrosanct tenet' which fiercely holds to "One Son Of God", we, on the other hand, will **state Truth** here.

So why is it important for global humanity as a whole to know this Truth? Are not all religions and beliefs regarded as having equal value today, for do not most also have gods too? References to "Sons of God" in the Christian sense would therefore surely be seen to have no apparent relationship with or to any other religious or cultural belief. However, even though ostensibly a "Christian subject", the, as-yet, *unseen ramifications for all of humankind* stemming from the question of non-recognition and/or denial of **The Two Sons of God** ultimately stands as *the* "Crucial Imperative" requiring unequivocal and timely recognition by *all* of global humanity.

The contentious nature of the subject matter in this particular Booklet will therefore obviously place it in direct opposition to the standard and long-held position of the mainstream Christian Churches. Why, then, have we gone out on a *seemingly* theologically-unassailable and therefore ostensibly-dangerous limb to proclaim unequivocally – and thereby directly challenge the stated position of the whole Christian world particularly – that there is not just *one* Son of God, *but Two*? If there has never yet been any *public* questioning of such a thing in the whole history of the Church, why bother now?

The answer is quite simple. As is the case of *all* the key questions in life; *either a thing is so, or it is not*! There is simply no other position that can be logically accepted. So must it be here. Therefore, *if* – *and the word if in this case is purely for the purpose of this immediate discussion* – there really is only One Son of God, Jesus, Who is to return and bring the Judgement and world peace etc., then the matter resolves itself.

This Booklet would then hold the dubious position of not only being very wrong but, against all perceived scholarly wisdom and academic knowledge from virtually all the Theological Colleges and Religious Studies Departments of the great Universities of the world would, in a rather foolish exercise expose the author of a "Two Sons of God" notion to considerable public ridicule.

No one in their right mind, therefore, would seriously consider publicly stating an idea that the academic world would

13

mock if there were not some exceptionally powerful motivation to do so. An extraordinarily strong "courage of conviction" would be required to actually *publish* such a view. For it is one that *seriously challenges* the supposedly infallible view of "the experts" – those with Doctorates/Ph.D's in Religious Studies, and the heads of the major Christian Churches. And, of course, not to mention the almost two billion Christian faithful who would also surely brand the whole notion ridiculous, perhaps even heretical.

The requisite "courage of conviction" on its own, however, would not be sufficient to question/challenge the current religious paradigm centred around Jesus as the **only** Son of God. Much more than simple courage is therefore required here. The key lies in certain and specific knowledge that not only reveals The Truth here, but profoundly reveals it to a point of Proclamation.

Historical examples of supposedly sacrosanct views of the Christian Church eventually being consigned to the rubbish heap of untruth are not at all uncommon. In any case, since *all* learning processes are actually evolutionary ones, so will it ultimately be with this new recognition. But it will be sooner rather than later.

Tragically, past centuries have borne witness to the torture and execution of radical dissenters who dared to even question the "infallible", official, Church position. A perfect example of "foolish infallibility" centred on the Graeco-Egyptian mathematician and geographer Ptolemy (A.D. 90-168) who proposed an astronomical system, readily accepted by the Church, that placed the earth at the center of the universe. In 1543, Polish Astronomer, Copernicus, published a description of the Solar System that correctly had the sun at the center. This new and radical "truth", however, was unacceptable to the Church. Copernicus was forced to recant.

From a point of immediate and outright rejection on pain of death, an absolute Truth can be *held at bay* for hundreds of years, then perversely embraced and defended as 'immutable truth' *by the very same*. The Church, as we all now know, **was very wrong**.

"Ruling authorities" – especially religious or scientific ones – do not usually readily-accept radical ideas that challenge *their* status quo, *even if the 'insight' is true.* In such situations there are only two possibilities for the governing elite. Deny it and continue to cling, at all costs, to the established "well of truth" deriving from the particular religious and/or academic position/s concerned, **or admit to being wrong**. In this case only *one* position, *one* action, would possess truly noble greatness – and honesty.

The obvious ramification of what is proposed here is therefore brutally simple. It states that **everything** previously believed and understood about Jesus being the **only** Son of God, **is completely wrong**. And the pages of this Booklet, especially, show why that is the Truth of it. Yes, there *are* references in The Bible that *purportedly* state that Jesus will *return*, but they are far outweighed by the greater number of statements by Him *warning* that Another – **The Other Son Of God** – would Come onto the earth! [**Son** actually means **Part**.]

A serious question arises for Christian readers who may cross the path of this analysis and derisively dismiss it as impossible rubbish – those who will not bother to even consider it *as* a possibility; and that is:
"What must the outcome be *if* this *is* the actual Truth?"
In reiteration, the word *if* is **only** for the purpose of this discussion, for we are postulating **an absolute and inviolable premise** here!
The clear, *connective premise*, therefore, is that Jesus **will not return to set physical foot on earth.** Hence the very sure Biblical warning that only the *few* – not the many hundreds of millions – would recognise.

In the final analysis, a denial of *any* ordination of **The Living Truth** from out of **The Divine Will** – even the *smallest* aspect – must ultimately fall back on all who so deny. A denial of the magnitude of the Truth surrounding **The Two Sons of God** would be *especially severe*, for it is tantamount *to a rejection of*: **The Divine Will Itself!** The great and inviolable Law: *"What a man sows, that shall he reap"* would ultimately return *dire consequences* in this case.

This Booklet thus offers the chance for many to awaken to one of the *greatest errors* of Christian teaching. However, as we stated at the head of this **Introduction**, it is not only the Christian world that needs to awaken to this monumental error, but **all** of humanity – including science and scientists.

In terms of the present degraded and poisoned state of the world, the crucial recognition of **"The Two Sons of God"** provides the key to understanding **Why** so many Nations, societies, religions and cultures are rapidly failing, and why that deterioration *cannot now be stayed.*

*   *   *   *   *

THE TWO SONS OF GOD

"Grace to you and peace, from **Him** who is, and who
was **and who is to come**; and from the seven Spirits
who are before **His throne**;
and from Jesus Christ,..."

(New American Standard Bible.)

"Blessing and peace to you from **the One** Who Is,
Who Was and **Who comes**; and from the seven Spirits which are before **His throne**;
and from Jesus Christ."[1]

(Revelation. 1:4-5, Fenton.
Emphases mine.)

That singular Scripture, *perhaps more than any other
in the entire Bible and all related religious writings*,
possesses the "Golden Key" to the clear reality of **The
Two Sons of God**! It needs only to be read with *an
open spirit* and without "religious fear" for the profound Truth of it to be ***intuitively recognised***.

---

[1] A key reason for the acceptance and promotion of Fenton's Bible by
"Crystal Publishing" may be noted in the small example represented
by that 'Scripture'. Fenton's hallmark trait throughout his translation is
his clear display of greater reverence for **The Godhead** through regular
and common use of **Capitals** when referencing **The Trinity**! This is
not the case with other Bible translators. **"Crystal Publishing"**, in
all its publications, unequivocally and unashamedly concurs with Fenton
on this most crucial matter.

The Two Sons of God! An unusual heading. Perhaps even blasphemous. Should we designate it a statement, or a question? Standard Christian beliefs generally accept an approaching end-time of great tribulation and destruction and the concomitant need for there to be the return of Jesus to Earth to, *ostensibly,* fulfil the revelatory prophecies from Biblical Scripture. Even Time magazine, Issue 1 July, 2002, devoted their lead story to this growing belief. Yet the contention that there *is* Another *other than* Jesus will, in all probability, be dismissed as ludicrous and impossible by many. However, let us keep an open mind and follow this key thread to its particular conclusion.

If we broadly trace the line of Religious Prophets and Truth-Bringers and the teachings they brought to Earth at their particular time in history – Lao-Tse, Zoroaster, Buddha and Mohammed, Moses and the Prophets etc., – we find revealed therein a spiritual/evolutionary continuum that leads to a particular level of knowledge and insight. Though gifted with exceptional spiritual insight and guided strongly in their tasks, what they could not give was the *greater* encompassing knowledge of the *wider* Creation. For it is not possible for *any* human being to *inherently know* that level of knowledge.

Thus it was that Jesus, The Son of God, brought a *more complete* knowledge of The Truth than had yet been given to mankind up to that point. In fact He brought the whole of The Truth **living within Him**, but humankind was too spiritually closed to fully recognise His Sacred Mission or accept and absorb all that He brought. Even those closest to Him, those who received more instruction than any others – His Disciples; even they were not sufficiently spiritually-matured to understand all that He *could* have given them. Aware that the ruling Jewish Religious Authority actively sought His death and that the time He would need to *fully* instruct the Disciples on the complete knowledge of The Truth would be denied Him, He began to speak of the time in the future when that *could* happen *for* them.

18

"I have still much more to tell you; but you are not yet able to bear it. When, however, the Spirit of Truth **Himself** comes, **He** will instruct you in all the truth:..."

(John 16:12-13, Fenton.
Emphases mine.)

So the time-line of the great Prophets and Truth-Bringers associated with the incarnation of Jesus onto the Earth plane reveal an almost evolutionary spiritual-knowledge path of Truth up to the present. And that is correct in its basic outline. The premise that this Work postulates absolutely unequivocally, therefore, is that *Jesus stands at the apex of Truth*, since **He Himself is a Living Part of It**. And He, as the **Part** thereof designated as not only **The Word** but also **"The Love of God"**, thus forever stands as:

One of The Two Sons of God!

If we did not state that reality as a living conviction in these pages, this Booklet would, of itself, be blasphemous. And would thereby serve to *corrupt* and *distort* the truth of:

The Living Word of God!

That we will not do since the purpose of this Work is to offer signposts to *the whole* of The Truth. The danger of denying that which is of The Living Truth Itself lies in the outworking of The Laws of Creation on those who so deny. That outworking rests completely and lawfully in The Law: *"What a man sows, that shall he reap."* Since there actually *are* **Two Sons of God**, a denial of this fact will ultimately visit its particular "reaping" too. Therefore, as we have designated Jesus as a Son of God and this Booklet is entitled, "**The Two Sons of God**":

Who, then, is The Other?

0.1   The Revelation of "The Other Son"

As background to our bold claim: In a *very compressed* journey in time, we need to look at the path and impact of Judaeo-Christian beliefs on both the civilised and the New Worlds long *after* the time of Christ. The rise and fall of the many civilisations of the "Ancient World", particularly those written about in the Old Testament, ultimately prepared the stage for the Message of Jesus to begin its journey out into the world. Initially, of course, across and out to the borders of the Roman Empire, but thence to its future dissemination to the wider world through the later European Empires. The general religious foundation of the latter is basically derived from the Judaeo-Christian ethos as outlined in The Bible. However, its entry into the European psyche to the present time saw it undergo many upheavals resulting in huge differences in meaning from the original simple and pure Teaching of Its Bringer: Jesus.

The religious authorities were not content to simply accept the clear Truth He brought but chose, instead, to erect huge monasteries and "schools of learning", behind which doors they could dissect His original Teachings. As a result of this long process of analysis and debate, the once-clear meanings underwent change, some subtle, some far more radical. What finally emerged from that fermenting crucible of *intellectual religiosity* differs vastly from the *Spiritual original* given by Jesus. Not only that, but for a time was also removed from the ordinary people. Thus, what little the masses were permitted to have, even that was used to enforce and maintain religious power over them by the few.

The sorry history of mankind testifies to the fact that through very especial "Called Ones", **Divine Will** many times strove to seed the great Truths in men. Men, however, unfortunately and *perversely*, subverted them all to just religions and/or splintered offshoots of. For the most part, therefore, they became institutions of earthly power, wealth and *religious* subjugation.

This dark volition can be readily traced through the mad, religious fervour of the Dark Ages and the equally insane Inquisition. The wealth and excesses of the Papacy seeded the wonderfully enlightened protestations of the great spiritual scholar Martin Luther who, in 1520, launched the Protestant Reformation. His opposition to the, then, entrenched religious view found a kindred soul in the English King, Henry VIII. By the Act of Supremacy in 1536, Henry effectively formed a new English Church and broke with Rome.

Later, via exploration and colonisation, the gradual expansion and consolidation of the European Maritime Nations to the New Worlds was effected. Thus, along with the export of European ideas and some of their criminals, went the zealous missionaries and their Christian religion in its more or less final, distilled form.

Whilst that was obviously an expansion of the European Empires, it was not at the same time an expansion of Spiritual Truth. What was exported to the new lands was far *less* spiritual than the original pure Teaching. The religious madness of the Dark Ages and the Inquisition had ensured that certain ideas of religious rigidity, formulated as dogma during those long centuries of bigotry and cruel torture, were henceforth retained as inviolable tenets of the new religious thinking. That is what arrived in the New World to challenge and then, for the most part, subjugate the peoples to whom it was usually forcibly introduced.

However, even though the "religion" had lost much of the essence of actual Spiritual Truth it was at least, in many ways, far more enlightened than anything some of the Indigenous peoples of the New World possessed. Thus, in accordance with their "divine mandate" as they believed it to be – **and paradoxically probably should have been** – European explorers and Missionaries carried *their* version of The Word, once delivered Spiritually-pristine from out of the mouth of Its Bringer, to many parts of the Earth.

What arrived in those far-off lands was therefore not truly a correct *interpretation* of the Teachings of Jesus as recorded

21

in The Bible. Religious scholars in great Universities and Theological Colleges today *still* argue and debate many points of religious disputation. Uncertain theoretical or theological argument should have no place in the dissemination of "The Living Word" given to humankind from One Whose Origin hailed from the very Source of that Word Itself! For any such wrong interpretation *must logically be* a dangerous transgression against the very **Creation-Laws** of **God**.

A radical statement concerning two Sons of God, then, would surely be described as too blasphemous to even consider, given that no past or present-day clergy or religious authority has *publicly* mooted this *possibility*. Yet, such radical assertions cannot be made without some relevant form of Biblical or Scriptural foundation to begin with. For that is the standard measure by which to anchor such a premise, at least in the world of Christian religion.

> In *this* Booklet, however, *other* avenues – of *exceptional knowledge* and *clear Spiritual Insight* –
> immeasurably assist us in our *factual premise*.

Despite the clearly contentious nature of what we are saying, we nevertheless urge well-meaning Christians and Biblical scholars to be sufficiently open-minded to at least *objectively* examine this matter. We categorically state, however, that we do not, in any shape or form, seek approbation or approval from any said religious or Christian Authority or Church anywhere to state what we assert herein. For, in reality, the debates that still rage among the "religious-learned" are simply the final end-excrescence of that process begun so many centuries ago, even pre-dating the Church-theology of Medieval Europe.

The relative times differ vastly of course in that today we possess far greater scientific knowledge about much more of the world. Unlike the Dark Ages when the Church held absolute power, a non-partisan Police Force and Judiciary today protect citizens who might wish to challenge the religious status-quo. To have asserted then what we assert here now would surely have resulted in charges of heresy and blasphemy, and thus a death sentence – one invariably preceded by cruel torture to try to force a recant.

As with most questions, however, the obvious reality is – as we must state often – that *either a thing is so, or it is not.* Particular historical times and events can *never* alter *that* particular truth. So is it with our radical assertion. Either there *are* Two Sons of God as we unequivocally state, or there is only one – Jesus. If, as we assert, there are two, then that clearly poses huge and fundamental questions for all Christians – and not least for the time that is referred to as "The Final Tribulation".

Let us therefore once more consult The Bible and the key Scriptures within that clearly *reveal* and *validate* the Truth about **"The Two Sons of God"**. And from *that* Truth in Biblical Scripture exactly around this crucial recognition, let us intuitively strive to understand the *monumental portent* and *far-reaching ramifications* of this *reality.*

The starting point of The Bible is, of course, The Book of Genesis. The general Christian belief about it all would probably aver that Genesis *seemingly* states that *in the beginning* there was only **GOD**. Thus a **One God** Who has existed from Eternity, and the darkness of a formless void. Nothing else. No life save that of **He, The Creator**. Further to that 'idea', therefore, it would be fair to say that most Christians believe that **God Himself** 'created the world and all in it'.

Yet John, the beloved of Jesus, makes a fundamentally more profound statement in the very first Verse of *his* Book. We know from New Testament Scripture that John and the other Disciples – who all lived literally cheek-by-jowl with Jesus – were given the greatest amount of knowledge that men had yet received about Creation, life and The Law. Since their Teacher was **The Son of God Himself**, we should surely expect that certain passages written by at least *some* of the Disciples *might just carry within them* far-reaching insights of tremendous spiritual import for *all* of humankind.

For the world of Christianity in this case, however, spiritual import of a potentially explosive nature. Thus we read in John, the beloved of Jesus, Chapter 1, Verses 1-3:

> "The **WORD** existed **in the beginning**, and the **WORD** was *with* **GOD** and the **WORD** *was* **GOD**.
> *He* was present *with* **GOD** at the beginning.
> **All** came into existence by means of *Him*; and nothing came into existence apart from *Him*."

> (Fenton Bible. Emphases mine.)

If we now analyse those passages with an open, objective and questing spirit and mind, we immediately see that *at the time when Creation came into being* there was not just GOD and the empty void, as Genesis might 'appear' to indicate. There was *Another – with* **GOD**! The obvious question automatically deriving from that crucial point must logically be:

Who was *"He Who was present with GOD...?"* Was 'He' Jesus, as is perhaps currently accepted? Or was 'He' the Other, to **Whom** we refer?

The key *insight* that must be grasped here is that *Whomever* it was that John referred to, was *present* *with* **GOD** '*at the beginning*'. Moreover, the use of the personal pronoun **He** is a clear pointer as to *Who this particular One actually is*. As a second vital pointer to the answer, the Scripture also clearly states that; *"...the Word that was with GOD..."* was the *"...He Who was present 'at the beginning'."* And that; *"...all came into existence by means of Him!"*

To reiterate the key point of that particular Scripture once more:

He Who was *with* **GOD** was **also** the **Word** *of* **GOD** too, and that **all** came into existence by means of **Him**! Such a simple statement is surely clear enough to understand, for there is no mystery here. As we have previously and seriously stressed, The Bible identifies **Who** that **"Other"** actually **Is**. The knowledge of **Who He** is thus clarifies/elucidates many points of religious contention.

Now to *further strengthen* our premise that He "Who was with God *at the beginning*" was the same He Who created "all things", all we need do is go to Verse 2 of Chapter 1 in Genesis. For the purpose of comparison and evaluation, we will quote from three different Bibles:

> "And the earth was without form, and void; and darkness was upon the face of the deep. And the *spirit* of God moved upon the face of the waters."
>
> (King James Bible.)

> "Now the earth was a formless void. There was darkness over the deep, and God's *spirit* hovered over the water."
>
> (Jerusalem Bible.)

> "But the Earth was unorganised and empty; and darkness covered its convulsed surface; while the *breath* of GOD rocked the surface of its waters."
>
> (Fenton.)

The unequivocal reference to a **'Creative Spirit'** in all three differently-sourced Scriptures clearly shows that it was not God Himself Who Created the "heavens and the earth", but **He Who was with Him!** The very fact that it is so written reveals that the ancient writers of the original texts *understood this clearly.* Of course, we should readily understand that Creation itself nevertheless proceeded only *according* to **GOD's Plan**, under *His Power and Authority*, but *through He* Who was *with* **GOD** as a *Part* of *Him.*

A note of caution should be sounded here. We should not attempt to interpret the *complete Creation-process* as involving just the *Earth* and its immediate, *material* inter-stellar environs. A clearly stupendous happening of colossal and *humanly-incomprehensible magnitude* would thereby be brought down to a superficial level of human-earthly *non-understanding*. Fenton's sub-heading provides the vital spiritual insight:

"The **First Creation** of the Universe by God..."

For the word "earth" does not refer solely to our earthly home but is symbolic of a *far larger Spiritual Reality.*[2]

The same basic reference to that **Other** With God can be found in both our main Bibles of reference and, indeed, in virtually all the different Bibles. So the same Scripture of John 1:1-3 in the King James Version reads:

"In the beginning was the **Word**, and the **Word** was *with* **GOD**, and the **Word** *was* **GOD**.
The *same* was in the beginning *with* **GOD**.
All things were made by *him*; and without *him* was not anything made that was made."

The Jerusalem Bible (1985 edition) states it similarly:

"In the beginning was the **Word**
the **Word** was *with* **GOD**
and the **Word was GOD**
He was *with* **GOD** in the beginning.
Through *Him* all things came into being
and not one thing came into being except through *Him*."

In order to more completely clarify this issue we should very carefully note that whilst **He** of **The Word** was *with* **GOD**, both **He** *and* **The Word** – *as an inseparable Part* – were *also* **GOD**. Yet whilst **He** is **The Word**, and **The**

---

[2]Fully explained in Chapter 2 of Parent Work: "The Origins of Man: Genesis and Science Agree!". [See end of Booklet for detailed clarification.]

Word *is* **GOD**, there is nevertheless a clear *demarcation* in the **'Divine Working'** *between* **He Who**, as the **Creative Will** *of* **GOD**, brought all things into being *through* **The Word**; – and **GOD** – out of **Whom He** of **The Word** *came*. Surely that is simple enough to understand...!

If we now track to certain other Bible passages where **Jesus** is similarly referred to as **The Word**, then *apparent* discrepancies do *appear* to develop. [Full clarification, however – given *by Jesus* to His Disciples – may be found in the following section **0.2**: **The Disciple's Confusion**. And in **0.3**: **"He" Who is "Enthroned"!**, further clarification from **The Revelation**.]

In *this* segment, from our two main reference Bibles, we will simply quote two Scriptures that have very unfortunately set in concrete for hundreds of millions the terribly erroneous belief of just **One Son**.

> "And the WORD became incarnate, and encamped among us – and we gazed upon His majesty, such majesty as that of a Father's only son – full of beneficence and truth."
>
> (John 1:14, Fenton.)

> "And the Word was made flesh and dwelt among us, (and we beheld his glory, the glory as of the only *begotten* of the Father,) full of grace and truth."
>
> (King James.)

> "No one has ever yet seen God; He has been made known by the only Son, Who exists in union with The Father."
>
> (John 1:18, Fenton.)

> "No man hath seen God at any time; the only *begotten* Son, which is in the bosom of the Father, he hath declared *him*."
>
> (King James. Emphases mine.)

27

Notwithstanding the *seemingly* ironclad meaning here, the word *begotten* in these particular Scriptures actually offers a pointer to the Truth of it all. For, ***in this case,*** **The One** who was *begotten* should not be regarded as **The One** who was *present **from the beginning** – **of Creation.***

Begotten: Past participle of ***beget***; – *'to cause to exist'.*

The Scripture therefore stands ***spiritually-correct.*** Jesus *was* the *only begotten* **Son** – ***after* The Creation.** For it was not **He** – as **The Love** of **GOD** – that *was* or *is* **The Creative Will** of **GOD. He,** as **The Love,** however, was also **The Word** too. Thus: **He** was ***that Part*** of ***The Word of GOD*** that *had* to incarnate on earth 2,000 years ago, if humankind was not to *fall* utterly and irretrievably. **— WHY? —**

As far back as the eighth century B.C., the prophet Isaiah *foresaw* the path that we of Planet Earth *would take.* The present-day state of it and its global societies clearly shows a calamitous and *rapidly-deteriorating situation.*

> "The earth also is *defiled* under the *inhabitants* thereof;
> because they have
> ***transgressed* the laws,**
> ***changed* the decrees,**
> ***broken* the everlasting covenant."**
>
> Therefore has the curse devoured the earth,
> and those that dwell therein are *desolate*:
> therefore the inhabitants of the earth are ***burned*,**[3]
> ***and few men left."***
>
> (Isaiah 24:5-6, Fenton. Emphases mine.)

It was therefore necessary for there to be the entry onto earth of **One** stronger than the prophets that preceded **Him.**

---

[3] The meaning of the term, *'burned'* – which continues to puzzle Bible scholars, theologians and scientists alike – is both clear and simple. We explain it in Section **0.4: Destruction by "Fire".**

They, for thousands of years, had continually warned the so-called 'chosen race' to heed **The Law**; but they, a 'stiff-necked people', would not.

> Thus **Jesus** came, ultimately for *all* humanity.
> For only **He** could explain **The Law** — **CREATION-LAW** — and thereby show the way back to The Truth, because the knowledge He bore was *Complete* and *Living* ***within Him.***

As previously stated: Aware that the ruling Jewish Religious Authority sought His death, Jesus realised two crucial things:

1. That the time He would need to *fully* instruct His Disciples on the *complete knowledge* of The Truth would be denied Him.

2. But also that even *they*, who were *closest* to Him, did not have the necessary spiritual maturity to *fully understand* the deeper knowledge He brought – the knowledge necessary to stem the downward path of a rapidly-falling humanity.

From then on He began to speak of the time in the future when that *would* happen. He thus began to speak of **The Other** Who would one day *bring to earth* the **ALL-TRUTH**. [Precisely to which this and all other works of Crystal Publishing point, and in which *is* found the *confirmatory knowledge* of **The Two Sons of God!**]

In an **Act of Love** totally incomprehensible to we of Planet Earth, the ***begetting*** of Jesus by **The Creator** from ***out of Himself*** stayed the complete and utter fall of humankind at *that* time. Through that process – and in a time-continuum that we human beings cannot hope to ***ever*** *even* ***begin*** *to understand* – may be seen the *sequence* of the *step-by-step* establishment of **The GODHEAD**.

＊　　　＊　　　＊　　　＊　　　＊

1. From Eternity: **GOD!** Alone.

2. At the *beginning* of the Creations: A *severance* of a
   Part of **Himself** as **The Creative Spirit** – **His Word**.

   "**All** came into existence by means of _**Him**_; and nothing came into existence apart from _**Him**_."

   Thus: **GOD** as a **Duality!**

3. After the disastrous 'Fall of Man': A *further* severance
   of a **Part** of **Himself** as **Jesus**: – **The Love of GOD**
   and **The Word of GOD** – to incarnate on earth to
   save a 'falling humanity'.

   Thus: **GOD** as a **Trinity. The TRIUNE GOD!**

＊　　　＊　　　＊　　　＊　　　＊

Paradoxically for global Christendom in the first instance,
but also for *all* religions and belief-systems and even science
in the second; the *key* to so many 'problem-questions' ultimately centers on the *knowledge of,* and *about,* **The Two
Sons!** – [Parts] – of GOD!.

Unfortunately, however, the 'default setting' of global Christendom to any notion that clashes with the 'official doctrine'
of *One Son only* is so locked in stone that even the most
catastrophic events will probably not be sufficient for this
most necessary awakening. Fear of change on the one hand,
and absolute certainty of their *One Son only* interpretation
on the other, will ensure – for the majority of Christians at
least – that Isaiah's clear prophecy *will come to pass.*

Now, what of this *other* "**SON of GOD**"? We know that
the Christian Churches – who *should* know The Bible – have
always spoken of only **One** Son of God, Jesus! And that He,
as The Living Word also, therefore brought the complete and

final Truth to mankind. He, as a Part of The Living Truth Itself, certainly *brought "the whole"*, living, **within Him**.

Due to humankind's spiritual immaturity at the time, however, that consequential inability to receive The Truth *fully* from Him meant that the *writings* of those who were closest to Him – His Disciples – are *incomplete* with regard to the *whole* that Jesus brought to earth at that time. The obvious ramification that such an assertion must logically presume is that The Bible, therefore, *does not contain the whole*.

The Apostle Paul provides the relevant insight in his 'Letter to the Corinthians'. We should carefully note that the words of Paul were written *after* the Crucifixion, and *after* the Outpouring which, according to some religious "scholars", *was* the watershed event that *would lead them* [the Disciples] into "all-Truth". Thus the time when Jesus would send The Holy Spirit.

The Church thus broadly accepts the Outpouring of The Holy Spirit at Pentecost as the fulfilment of a key prophecy of Jesus i.e., "...to send the Helper, the Comforter, The Spirit of Truth after His departure". Jesus is recorded as stating, however, that The Holy Spirit "...will reprove the world of sin". The word, 'reprove', clearly means to reprimand, to admonish, to reproach. The Outpouring of The Holy Spirit, however, has not resulted in this event even two thousand years later.

It therefore unequivocally refers to that which this specific Booklet addresses. *It refers to the Coming of The Son of Man Who is also The Spirit of Truth/The Holy Spirit.*

Against this fact, some may cite the words of Matthew 12:32. (New American Standard Bible.):

> "Anyone who speaks a word against The Son of man will *be* forgiven, but anyone who speaks against The Holy Spirit will *not be* forgiven, either in this age or the age to come."

The contention may thus arise that, as per the above, Jesus *seemingly* differentiates between The Son of Man and The

Holy Spirit. Clearly, there are different ways of interpreting that Scripture. One could say that even if The Son of Man and The Holy Spirit are one and the same Person, speaking a single word against Him may be forgiven, but *continually speaking* against The Holy Spirit will not result in forgiveness. This clarifying interpretation becomes more plausible when one considers a different translation of the same Scripture from **Fenton**:

> "And if one gives expression to a thought against The Son of Man, it shall be forgiven him, but if one shall speak insultingly of The Holy Spirit it shall not be forgiven him, neither at the present time, nor in the future."

Here there is a clear difference between the phrase, "gives expression to a thought" versus "shall speak insultingly". The reader must spiritually-perceive and thus enter into the *true* sense of the words whilst understanding that the designations, Spirit of Truth, Holy Spirit and Son of Man – whilst seeming to be separate entities – are nevertheless: **One and The Same!**

We can perhaps better understand the *non-forgiveness* aspect of the Scripture which pertains to the title, "**The Holy Spirit**", if we relate it to that **Part** of **The Son of Man** which *is* **The Holy Spirit** *as* the **Creative Spirit** – **THE WILL** – *of* **GOD**. Thus **He** Who brought all things into being *through* **The Word.** We, also brought into being and gifted conscious life by the very same **Creative Spirit**, should therefore understand the strict requirement to not transgress the **Divine Commandment:**
"Thou Shalt Not Take The Name Of The Lord Thy God In Vain."
Thus, in reiteration: **He** of the **Word** Who was *with* **GOD** is also **He** Who **Is** **The Word** *of* **GOD**.

Notwithstanding the obvious Spiritual Power that must have

been experienced by those present at "The Outpouring" at Pentecost, Paul states very clearly:

> "For we know *in part*, and we prophesy *in part*. But when that *which is perfect is come*, then that which is *in part* shall be *done away*."

> (1 Corinthians 13:9-10, King James.)

Fenton translates the same passages thus:

> "For we know *imperfectly*, and we teach with *imperfection*; but when the *perfect* arrives, the *imperfect* will *become useless*."

And The Jerusalem Bible says:

> "For our *knowledge* is *imperfect,* and our prophesying is *imperfect*; but once *perfection* comes, all *imperfect* things will *disappear*."

> (All emphases mine.)

Simple logic must lead us to the obvious conclusion that Paul could not have been referring to Jesus Himself as the *"part"* or the *imperfect,* for He, Whose Origin was The Divine, was *complete* in *Knowledge* and *Perfection*. In all of Paul's ministry, nothing to the contrary was ever so stated by him. In any case, it would be ludicrous to try to argue that the Teachings of Jesus – as The Son of God – could be *done away* with, *become useless*, or *disappear*. Paul certainly knew that, as did the Disciples.

For Matthew (24:35 Fenton, parenthetic addition mine) records Jesus stating in admonishing warning that:

> "The heaven and the earth may fade away; [*disappear*], but My Declarations [The Truth] will never pass away."

33

As previously examined, theologians and Bible scholars could be forgiven for believing that The Outpouring was, after all, the event where The Holy Spirit gave the "*complete and perfect*", the All-Truth, to the Disciples. For the strength of the happening was such that they all spoke in tongues and became seeing. Yet a simple analysis of it all points to a very different conclusion; a conclusion that Paul understood quite clearly. Therefore, if Jesus was not *"the part"* – and He surely was not the *imperfect* – then Who or what was Paul referring to? Who, therefore, would bring the Perfect, and when?

0.2   The Disciples' Confusion

That answer lies in the following Scriptures given by *Jesus* in reply to questions from His Disciples regarding the Endtime. The singularly-strong aspect here is the clear statement that **The One to come** would instruct in *all* the *Truth*, meaning that Jesus *had not done so*. In other words, what He was *able to give for that particular point* in human spiritual evolution and have it at least basically understood, was just a *part* of the whole, *not* the *complete* thing.

In necessary reinforcement, this is so stated in John 16:12:

> "I have still much more to tell you; *but you are not able to bear it.*"

So: Even though instructed by The Son of God Himself to a far deeper level of knowledge than certainly any other human beings to that time, the greater degree of understanding that humankind *still required* could not be imparted to the Disciples *then*. It was simply too much for them to understand or assimilate.

Therefore another, **The Other**, would have to come and bring *all* **The Truth**.

> "...because if **I** do not depart, the Helper will certainly not come to you; but when **I** depart, **I** will send *Him*

34

to you. *He*, on *His* coming, will bring conviction to the world..." — — And also:

"When, however, the Spirit of Truth *Himself* comes, *He* will instruct you *in all the truth*... *He Himself* will honour Me..."

(John 16:7-8 & 13-14, Fenton.
Emphases mine.)

Matthew describes the key sign which will reveal the fact that The Eternal Mediator is – *or has already been* – on Earth. The following Scriptures not only add more Biblical weight to our premise, but they further illustrate the fact that Jesus does not refer to Himself in the first person but clearly infers that there really *is* Another.

"...and then will appear the signal of the Son of Man in the sky. And **He** will send out **His** messengers – and they will collect all **His** chosen..."

(Matthew 24:30-31, Fenton.)

Matthew, in 25:31, offers another powerful statement from Jesus in support of the **Other One**. Again, He *does not say* **"I"** will do this or that, but that the **Other One – He, The Son of Man** – will fulfil it!

"But when the Son of Man appears in **His** Majesty, and all **His** angels with **Him**, then **He** will take **His** seat upon the throne of **His** Majesty; and collect all nations before **Himself**."

In that particular Scripture, as in many others, we would at least expect Jesus to say, **"I** will collect all Nations before **Me."** – if **He Himself** was to fulfil that role at the End-time. Yet that is not what **He** says, even though instructing and enlightening His Disciples as to what to expect then! Further Scriptural quotes clarify our premise. From John 14:26 and Luke 18:8, respectively.

"...but the helper, the Holy Spirit, Whom the Father will send... **He** will teach you everything".

"When the Son of Man comes, however, will **He** find this faith upon the earth?"

Two examples from The Jerusalem Bible provide more anchorage for our premise:

"...proved by my going to the Father and your *seeing Me no more*".

"I came from the Father and have come into the world, and now *I leave the world to go to the Father.*"

(John 16:10 and 16:28)

A strong example of what we contend can be found in Mark, [Fenton] Chapter 8, Verse 38.

"If *anyone*, however, is ashamed of **Me** and of **My** teachings in this adulterous and wicked race, then will the Son of Man be ashamed of *him*, when **He** comes with the holy angels in the majesty of **His** Father."

In this example, Jesus does not say; "...when **I** come... in the majesty of **My** Father." as He surely would have if He was to fulfil that future role. Such statements reveal that Jesus knew He would *not* return to the Earth as the "Eternal Mediator", and that He knew Who *would*. He therefore prepared the Disciples, **and thus mankind through their writings**, to expect such an event.

The clear inference in all of these Scriptures is that the use of the personal pronoun, **He**, denotes an *actual* person in the same way that **Jesus** was an *actual person*. And, moreover, would be **The One** Whom *Jesus would send*, but only *after His* [Jesus's] *own departure*.

The "Second Coming of Christ" has been "accepted" as a non-negotiable event for centuries now by virtually all Christian groups. The ostensible sureness of that happening as espoused by Global Christendom, however, is clearly thrown into question if we assess particular Scriptural statements brutally-objectively. For *if* **The Other** *is* to come – the word-concept *if* only being used for the purposes of this discussion of this moment – such a crucial event must ultimately shake the very foundation of *all* religions and *all* science. In fact it would impact on every facet of what it means to be a human being resident in *Subsequent Creation* at this time. And whether one is on Earth or passed from it is irrelevant.

The quandary for the global Christian community of *if, or should, or when* centred on the *ostensible* return of Jesus and not any thought for the Coming of **The Other**, presupposes the probability that Christianity/humankind, in general disbelief anyway, will ignore it and continue to embrace, instead, totally different and therefore *wrong* concepts. The end result will surely not then be as Christians, particularly, might hope or imagine.

Even though global Christendom firmly believes that Jesus "will return", how would such a "return" occur and for what purpose, given that **The Other** – the actual **Bringer of the All-Truth** – **would be here on Earth with that [His] All-Truth?** Is this another Bible mystery? No! Not with the complete knowledge contained *within* that **All-Truth**.

What we do have, however, is a **new knowledge** of a **"dual working"** of **Two** **Sons of God**. [You, reader, might be surprised to learn that a dual working *is precisely stated* in **The Book of Revelation**. That particular Scripture, along with others of revelatory insight, is detailed in the following Section: "**He Who is Enthroned**".]

If we now look to The Revelation in Fenton's Bible, Chapter 1 Verses 4 and 5, [our defining introductory quote to this Booklet] we should singularly note, in strict objectivity, the strong statement of differentiation between **The Two**.

> "Blessing and peace to you from **the One** Who Is, Who Was and **Who comes**; and from the seven Spirits which are before **His throne**; — **and** from Jesus Christ."

It is patently clear from the above Scripture that there is more than just one **"One"**. Moreover, the strongly denoted *separative-conjunction* **"and"** draws a clear line of demarcation between Jesus **and** — **The Other – The One** — "Who Is, Who Was and **Who Comes**"! This key Scripture reveals the fact very clearly for: "...the seven spirits are **before His Throne...**" And it is the throne of "**He Who Comes...**" Thus, in very necessary, repetitive-reinforcement in this crucial case: **The One Enthroned – is – The One Who Comes!**

He Who Comes, therefore, ***cannot possibly be* GOD, The Creator, Himself**, because it is **not** **"The Almighty" Who comes to Earth.** [*If it were even possible to begin with, the whole of the "Material Worlds" – in all its humanly-incomprehensible immensity – would be utterly consumed by His Power.*] For how could He possibly be The Eternal Mediator Who would thus have to, very illogically, stand as the link *between* humankind *and Himself*? That role belongs to The One appointed for the Task. The One "Who is, Who Was and **Who Comes**" – **The Alpha and the Omega – The Word of God Who exists**: the **All-ruler!**

> Therefore **The One Enthroned** is thus **"The One"** Who Comes as: **The Eternal Mediator, The Holy Spirit, The Son of Man. He** is that **Part** out of **GOD** Who Comes as **HIS Will.** So it is *not* Jesus Who Comes, for **He** is in the *immediate presence* of ***The One Who does.***

Despite the crystal-clear logic of our explanations, we would yet be safe in commenting that the general, broad interpretation by many of the mainstream Christian Churches of the crucial message to John about "Who is to come" would teach that Jesus in the presence of **The One Enthroned** *would be interpreted* as Jesus in the immediate presence of **GOD** Who, of course, would naturally be Enthroned. However, as is brutally clear from the very logic inherent in the

whole discourse, and which we will restate *again*:
The One Who *is* Enthroned, is **also** *The One Who Comes*, so therefore **cannot possibly** be **GOD!** For "HE" is "**THE ALMIGHTY**" Who cannot *descend* to the Earth, and is thus **THE ONE** Whom;
"...**no man hath seen** *at any time*"!

Therefore, in logic brutal and clear, the *very fact* that the blessed recipient of this vision in the first place *could behold* **The One** *upon* **The Throne**, *automatically tells us* that **He** Who can be *seen* **Enthroned** *cannot possibly be* **THE CREATOR**. The One seen **Enthroned above All Creation** and designated as **The Lord** – is the **Living, Creative**, aspect of **God**.

The entry onto the Earth of **The One Who Comes** with the complete and Perfect Whole of the All-Truth would thus ultimately fulfil the prophecies of Jesus and statements of Paul in that it would render any accumulated knowledge and belief, past and present, individual and collective, religious and scientific – *that did not perfectly accord with it* – irrelevant, and therefore useless. That is exactly the *"in part"* that shall be *"done away"*; and the *"imperfect"* that will *"become useless"*. It is when *"all imperfect things will disappear"*.

Thus it is actually for *this present era of humanity* with its concomitant spiritual and technological development that the *whole*, the *complete*, the *perfect,* was intended for. And the **One Who Comes** is **The One** *Who* would bring it. The same **Who**, as **The Spirit of Truth**, Jesus was to send. Moreover, the **All-Truth** that He would bring would speak *of* Jesus, as we have previously stated.

A very crucial message of Jesus to His Disciples clearly reveals the obvious fact that He is telling them about **The Other Son — Who is to Come**. The constant reference and emphasis in the personal pronoun here unequivocally shows that **The One** about Whom He is talking is not some vapourous or disembodied entity, but Someone – just as Jesus had to be – Who would be **present** in a **physical body on Earth**, BUT **at a future time**.

The simple statement: **"He Himself will honour Me"**, tells it all very, very clearly in the fullness of the complete Scripture.

> "I have still much more to tell you; but you are not yet able to bear it. When, however, the Spirit of Truth <u>Himself</u> comes, <u>He</u> will instruct you in *all* the truth: for <u>His</u> utterances do not proceed from <u>Himself</u>; but just what <u>He</u> learns <u>He</u> will declare, and the events that are coming <u>He</u> will announce to you.

<u>He Himself</u> will honour <u>Me</u>.

> ...because what <u>He</u> receives from <u>Me</u>, <u>He</u> will transmit to you. All that the Father possesses is Mine: that is why I said, 'It is of <u>Mine</u> that <u>He</u> takes and transmits to you.' Only a little while, and you will not see Me; and again a little while, and you shall see Me."[4]

(John 16:12-16, Fenton.
All emphases mine.)

The two thousand year time-frame since the time of Christ has permitted us the luxury of greater understanding and awareness of a far wider world than the people in His time could ever have known. Because of the greater level of overall knowledge now taught as a matter of course through scientific Disciplines, Institutions of "higher" learning and in the general education systems today, the presupposition should therefore be that we are now also sufficiently *spiritually* equipped to recognise this complete whole when it arrives. And thus similarly recognise **The Bringer** of it. **The Spirit of Truth; The Holy Spirit; The One Who Comes!**

---

[4]We may note in the last sentence the preparation for the Disciples of the impending event of His earthly death – "and you will not see Me" – and after "a little while" when He would rise in His non-earthly body, when – "you shall see Me".

Since it is *our present time* that is spoken of, the spiritual faculty within each one of us *should*, therefore, at least *intuitively* perceive that such an event is imminent – *or has possibly already occurred*. Yet, almost the whole of the Prophetic utterings of Jesus and the Prophets within the pages of The Bible clearly show that the majority of mankind *will miss the moment*; will *not be awake at the time*.

If we do *not recognise* in time, if we miss that moment, if we simply refuse to accept – *even if it should pass before us* – what happens then? If we stubbornly cling to what we presently believe out of fear of letting go, what will that mean for the one who has missed it, or for the one who is asleep? In turn, what will it mean for global humanity, *if the majority of the world's people – including, therefore, most Christians – are blind to the happening?*

Then, as we intimate, *if* there has not been sufficient recognition and spiritual growth and change in humankind:

> "...all the tribes of the earth shall mourn..."

> (Matthew 24:30, Fenton.)

> "...then too all the peoples of the earth will beat their breasts..."

> (Matthew 24:30,
> New Jerusalem Bible.)

Matthew, Chapter 24, offers key pointers to this question of whether Jesus was or is to return. For example, from verses 3-5:

> Afterwards, when He was resting upon the Mount of Olives, His disciples approached Him privately, asking, "Tell us when this will be; and what is the signal of Your presence, and the completion of this age." "Take care," said Jesus, in reply to them, "that none may deceive you. For many will come in My Name, asserting "I am the Messiah", and will lead many astray."

41

Verses 23 to 25 offer more indications.

> Then if any should say to you, "Look! the Messiah is
> 'here', or 'there' do not believe it. For false prophets
> will make their appearance; and will give out great
> and terrible omens, so as to mislead, if possible, even
> the chosen. However, *I have forewarned you*."

Here Jesus surely indicates that many would pretend to
be Him and that the Disciples would need to exercise the
greatest possible degree of alertness and spiritual discernment
when the time for the entry of The Son of Man onto the Earth
arrived. That logically means that The Son of Man, The
Eternal Mediator, *would be here when many false prophets
would claim to be Jesus*. Historically, messianic claims are
nothing new. It would be fair to say, however, that the 20th
century probably saw the public emergence of perhaps more
false messiahs than ever previously recorded. And, of course,
many are alive and well in the 21st century too. So is He
here? **If so, where?**

Despite the fact that we *can* find passages where Jesus
apparently indicates He will return, it is **The Son of Man
Who is to Come as The Eternal Mediator** – as Jesus clearly states. For too many other statements by Him
show clear reference to the **Other** Whom **He** is to send. If
it was unequivocally and absolutely certain that Jesus *was*
The One Who Comes, then we would surely expect that
all statements, references, Scriptures, inferences etc., would
carry the **"I"** and not the **"He"** so clearly evident in so many
places.

If it *was* so absolute, as Christian thinking today states
so emphatically, then surely the men who were closest to Him
– even though not fully understanding all that He gave them
– would have written so in every case. However, that is not
what we read, for that is not what they wrote. **For that
is not what He told them in this case!** Why are we
so emphatic about this exact aspect? Quite simple: A *very
telling* point has been missed here. It is this:

42

The very fact that the Disciples did *not under-stand* Jesus on this issue, yet **nonetheless still** recorded the "**HE**" *more often* than the "**I**", must clearly presuppose that they really did *faith-fully chronicle for posterity what they were told by Him — despite their 'confusion'.* Otherwise, human nature being what it is, they would all have interpreted His words to replicate what *they believed* He meant; that The Son of God and The Son of Man Whom Jesus spoke about so often towards the end of His Ministry, were one and the same – i.e., **He**, their **Master**. Notwithstanding their confusion – and as we have noted in this Work – the Gospels nonetheless reference the "**HE**", The Other, *"Who is to Come"*, in many places.

We know there exists in Christendom the very prevalent *belief* that **The Bible** in its *entirety* is **The Word of God** given through *'inspiration without deviation'*. We also know that The Bible records Jesus as telling His Disciples they were *not ready* to receive all the knowledge **He** carried *within*, because they would not understand it. Should that not sound a note of warning to Christianity? We certainly think so. Why? For a very long time now global Christendom has conditioned itself to faithfully believe that The Bible provides an *absolute* and thus *non-negotiable* tenet: **One Son of God, Jesus**, Who is to return as "**The Eternal Media-tor**". Yet that especial Work does not at all agree with what has now become a sacrosanct Church-ordination. So where lies the 'without deviation inspirational aspect' which must, by Christian definition at least, *never be questioned*?

An interesting yet problematic quandary for Christendom therefore rears its unwelcome head here, for the very Scrip-tures we quote and the obvious analyses and conclusions aris-ing from them reveal a tenet that simply "does not stack up". So which parts of the relevant Scriptures, messages, writings, admonitions etc., should we accept – or ignore – in order "to make it fit"?

If Jesus really is to return as The Eternal Mediator, why did the Disciples not change their texts to read accordingly and thus use the **I**, solely, in their collective Gospels and writings? Moreover, why did all later translators and interpreters *also not change* that wording? Surely, in terms of human language, this is nothing more than very simple and basic grammatical expediency – for all languages must clearly differentiate between **I** and **HE**. If that were not the case normal discourse would be severely hampered, if not impossible.

Perhaps, on this most crucial issue, it really is a case of **The Divine Will** ensuring that *despite* so much *non-understanding throughout history*, The Bible actually does *"tell it like it is"* with regard to **The HE** Who is **The One** to set foot on Earth at the Divinely-ordained hour. Global Christendom *should* take *serious note* of the absolute truism proffered by the Danish philosopher, Kierkegaard:

> 'It is not the Truth that lies with the *masses*, but
> the untruth. The *crowd* is the 'untruth'.'

The validity or otherwise of the Gospels of the Four Evangelists has been the subject of much scrutiny and debate by Bible scholars and theologians for centuries now. It is clear that the original writings, or perhaps more specifically the original words given to the Disciples from Jesus, underwent much change and editing through many translations, but also through the personal or religious bias of various scribes and translators. The present format of The Bible, however, was primarily determined by Constantine, the first Christian Roman Emperor, who decreed to the, then, Church hierarchy the more-or-less final form that it now takes. Riding on the back of Constantine's directive, powerful, at times tyrannical, Church leaders who believed themselves to be spiritually-enlightened and infallible scholars, held steadfastly to that decree. Recent researchers have seized upon these historical facts to thus question the actual validity of those Gospels.

The co-authors of "The Holy Blood And The Holy Grail" make much of this to lend credence to their particular premise. It is surely impractical and illogical, however, to believe that the Disciples of Jesus would report everything that transpired during their association with Him in *exactly* the same way. They were chosen *not* because of their *sameness* but because of their *differences*. They would therefore likely report events in the short yet hugely eventful Ministry of Jesus in historically volatile times differently from each other. Certain events would no doubt obviously impact more decisively on some than on others.

So the very fact that they apparently *did* report things slightly differently, with one or two clearly important events omitted from *some* Gospels, should not detract from the main and critical message ultimately contained *within the four Gospels*. Rather, it should be seen as a convincing insight into a much broader sweep of their overall connection and association with Jesus. Thus what they were tasked to pass on to the world.

Therefore, despite the obvious fact that the Evangelists were very different individuals from diverse educational and working backgrounds, The Books of the Four are *remarkably consistent* with regard **to what we are postulating here**. They no doubt made mistakes and perhaps did not report exactly all that transpired, and they clearly did not understand all that Jesus told them, according to *their* record of **His** statements. However, one could assume that if there were *huge* and *irreconcilable differences* and not simply minor ones in terms of what they were told by Jesus – or believed they were told, or grossly misinterpreted what they were told or heard – then we would surely see evidence of that in their individual writings.

That is clearly not the case, however. In fact the *consistency* with which references to **The Other**, obviously from Jesus Himself – *for where else could they have possibly gotten it from* – faithfully reproduced in the four Gospels by the four Evangelists clearly indicates, in our view, a singularly important aspect of what Jesus was trying to impart. And the four, in essence, recorded exactly that.

Despite the sureness that the global Christian Church in its many guises confidently exudes about the "non-negotiable return of Jesus", the facts we outline here show that such a scenario *will* ultimately turn out to be **not the case**! The *actual reality* for the greater majority of humankind is very clearly spelt out in the Scriptural warnings from Jesus – He Who would send **The Other Who Is to Come**. As a further problem for such believers, any entry of The Eternal Mediator onto the Earth surely poses huge and fundamental problems for all Christian groupings that accept the validity of the return of "someone". For in the first place:

"Who will He come to?"

Since only cool, clear objectivity offers the key to a logical interpretation of prophetic Scripture, not emotive Christian religiosity, then we should well understand the obvious fact that the **All-ruler** – the **Alpha** and the **Omega, The Eternal Mediator** – *must* and *will* stand far above such earthly ideas as diverse religious denominations. He therefore *will not*, and indeed *cannot*, ally Himself to any one group or Church. To put it bluntly, such a notion *is just plain silly*!

A singularly important aspect of "His" Coming would require it to be strongly linked to the appointed time and thus to any indicative signs that *might* precede this event. As previously stated, the key requirement must surely be the **CRUCIAL RECOGNITION** that such an event was imminent. *Or perhaps had already taken place*, and thereby been *completely missed by most*.

So, from the Disciples of Jesus, from those who lived with Him, who heard His Words and bequeathed their experiences to posterity, we offer a few more of His admonitions. Warnings to be fully awake and alert, to not get so bogged down in everyday worldly matters or pleasures that the spirit inside each of us falls asleep and misses the moment forever. Should this event not be recognised, that non-recognition will not stop the tribulatory effects that will be associated with it.

For the arrival of **The Son of Man** as **The Eternal Mediator** *heralds the beginning of the complete collapse of all distorted religious beliefs of the peoples of Earth, along with all wrong science.*

> "On account of this, be ready! because it may be that the Son of Man will appear at a time you do not expect."
>
> "Be you also ready; for it may be that the Son of Man will come at an unexpected moment."
>
> (Luke 12:40 and 44, Fenton.)
>
> "You too must stand ready, because the Son of Man is coming at an hour you do not expect."
>
> (Same Scripture – The Jerusalem Bible.)
>
> "Keep guard, therefore, for you know not what hour your Lord may come."
>
> (Matthew 24:42, Fenton.)

And in the parable of the ten thoughtless bridesmaids who were shut out of the wedding, Jesus admonishes and warns humankind to be alert and awake to this return.

> "Therefore keep awake; because you know neither the day nor the hour when the Son of Man will come."
>
> (Matthew 25:13.)

Paul's contribution to this reality is well stated in 1st Thessalonians 5:1-2.

"But about the times and the seasons, brethren, there is no need for writing to you: for yourselves know well enough that the day of the Lord comes like a thief at night."

(Fenton.)

Luke, 21:34-36 Fenton, gives a particularly strong warning about the crucial need to not miss the time or the moment. (Emphasis mine):

"But take care of yourselves, for fear your hearts should be loaded with debauchery, and drunkenness, ***and business cares***,[5] and that day come swiftly upon you like a snare; for thus it will come upon all dwelling upon the face of the earth. Watch, therefore, at every season, offering prayer; so that you may be prepared to escape all the coming calamities, and take your stand in the presence of the Son of Man."

The Jerusalem Bible notates the same passages thus:

"Watch yourselves, or your hearts will be coarsened with debauchery and drunkenness and the cares of life, and that day will be sprung on you suddenly, like a trap. For it will come down on every living man on the face of the earth. Stay awake, praying at all times for the strength to survive all that is going to happen, and to stand with confidence before the Son of Man."

*   *   *   *   *

It is vitally important to understand ***why*** Jesus so strongly warned His Disciples to yet ***prepare*** for the ***entry*** of The Son of Man *at the end of the times.* Since He did not mean in ***His*** lifetime

---

[5]Surely here is the greatest warning yet to the corporate world and its financiers, exchange-rate manipulators, share-market fanatics and all of similar ilk who elevate the *god-corporate* and the *god-financial* before all else. **"For what will it profit a man if he should gain the whole world and forfeit his life?"** [...lose his soul?]

or even shortly thereafter – **because we have had 2000 years of history since** – *how, then,* could the Disciples watch and wait for such an event *if they all followed the natural path of life into earthly death as they obviously all did around that time?*

The answer lies in the overarching knowledge *inherent within* "<u>**Creation-Law**</u>", explained in the Parent Work: i.e., Chapter 3; ['**The Spiritual Laws: The Necessary knowledge**']. In this case, namely **The Law of Rebirth**. Therein lies the answer *immutability in concert with the spiritually lawful processes and inviolable outworking for all human beings that is the sure aftermath of the First Death*, and the subsequent paths that *must* be taken **thereafter** – to either *life eternal*; or to the *Second Death*.

*   *   *   *   *

The warning to the Disciples to 'watch and wait' meant that they should be alert and awake to the signs which would herald the *arrival* of **'The Other'** far in *the future*. The clear admonition of Jesus to them of His words, "*I have forewarned you...*", was to prepare them for a future end-time of great confusion. *For at least some would need to be on Earth <u>again</u>, to stand in the presence of 'The Other'.* However, it was not just His Disciples to whom Jesus addressed the warning. It was to all of humanity then and now; for this time – today! For this is the era of **The Son of Man** and thus The Judgement for all!

A primary statement given by Jesus to His Disciples about the end-times indicates this clearly.

"Verily I say unto you, This generation *shall not pass away* till all be fulfilled."

(Luke 21:32 King James.
Italics mine.)

From The Book of Matthew, 24:34-35, Fenton:

> "I tell you indeed, that this generation *shall not pass away* until all these arrive. The heaven and the earth may fade away; but My declarations will never pass away."

Thus the generation of that time, those responsible for His murder, would all have to be back on the Earth to stand before the *Living Truth* of **The Son of Man**. Either to *pass into life* – *if* there had been sufficient "good works" for expiation of the deed since – or to *pass from life*; to pass away in the "second death", if there had not. All generations before and since would similarly be required to face their own individual wrongs, whilst in the same period also experiencing the destruction of all the wrong that humankind had collectively produced – to also either *pass from life* or *pass into life*.

One more warning – and one that surely applies to Western societies today!

> "And as in the days of Noah, so will also be the appearance of the Son of Man. For as they were, in the days before the flood, eating and drinking, marrying and giving in marriage, until the day arrived for Noah to enter the ark, and ***they would not understand*** until the flood came ***and carried all away***."

> (Matthew 24:37-39, Fenton.
> Emphases mine.)

This is that period. It *is* the time of that **prophesied fulfilment!**

> "And there will be signs in the sun, and moon, and stars; and upon the earth nations in despair, as when in terror of the roaring and raging sea; men expiring from fear, and apprehension of what is coming upon the world:..."

> (Luke 21:25-26, Fenton.)

Continuing on from that very necessary explanation, let us learn more about this singularly momentous issue. For if the full import of it is truly recognised and really understood, that recognition and understanding could then open a door that would greatly assist us *to pass into life.*

In this part of *our* revelation it is essential to stress the fact that The Bible regularly notes *two different references* to *two* particular **"Names"** and *two* respective **"Titles"** in various places within its pages. The general assumption has been that both contrasting titles referred to the same **One** – Jesus! Yet, firstly, we have the two different "Titles": **The Son of God *and* The Son of Man!** Secondly, we have the two different "Names" – **Jesus *and* Imanuel!** The Christian Churches, however, generally teach They are one and the same.

The Gospel of Luke, 1:31-32 and 35, offers a prime example of what we are saying. The message of the Archangel, Gabriel, to Mary is very clear.

> "And listen: you shall conceive and give birth to a Son; and you shall give Him the name of **Jesus**."

> "...and therefore the holy result shall be called **Son of God**".

Conversely, Matthew's unfortunate mistake has bequeathed a legacy which has misled many successive generations to the present day. For in Chapter 1 he writes that prior to the birth of Jesus, Joseph, knowing he was not the father, was nevertheless directed by a messenger of the Lord to accept Mary as his wife. In Verse 21 Matthew states:

> "And she will give birth to a Son **and you shall name Him Jesus**..."

Then in Verse 23, (Fenton's Capitalisation, emphases mine), Matthew, perhaps out of his own beliefs and/or lack of sufficiently clear spiritual understanding, later writes:

"Now all this took place so that the statement of the Lord, as recorded by His prophet, might be fulfilled: BEHOLD, THE VIRGIN SHALL CONCEIVE, AND GIVE BIRTH TO A SON; AND THEY SHALL CALL HIS NAME **EMMANUEL**, which, when translated, means THE GOD AMONG US."

Joseph, however, *did not* name the child **Imanuel** but, in accordance with the *instructions* of the "messenger of the Lord", named Him **Jesus**.

Therefore, what should be understood here is the very crucial fact that whereas the *messenger* of **The Lord** clearly proclaimed **Jesus** as **The Son of God**; Isaiah [7:14] was the prophet who prophesied, and thus *proclaimed*, **Imanuel** as **The Son of Man: The Eternal Mediator!**

Matthew has very wrongly attempted to make two into one for the references relating to this truly 'dogma-shattering' *revelation* in Chapter 1 of *his* Gospel are simply illogical. Had he received a personal visit from a messenger from Above who stated otherwise, Matthew would surely have written so. In quoting Isaiah he clearly does not recognise his own mistake, and neither have many since. He has therefore unfortunately bequeathed a huge error to posterity because his use of the Scriptures here make no sense. They serve only to confuse and cloud a very vital issue.

0.3 "HE" Who Is "Enthroned"!

To fully explain the meaning of *this* sub-Section, we need to now carefully examine particular Scriptures from 'The Book of Revelation' – that Book of which no word is to be altered – handed down to us by *the John* whom Jesus proclaimed as the "none greater among men". If we very carefully note the following references, we can readily see that there are, indeed: **TWO!**

Chapters 4, 5, 6 and 7 state this reality. So, in Revelation 4:2, John observed:

"...a throne in the heaven, and upon the throne an Occupant".

In the previous Section we established the *Biblical* fact that **The One Who Comes** is **'Enthroned'**! And in Revelation 4:9, those in attendance:

"...give praise, honour and thanks, to the Occupant of the Throne, Who lives for ever and ever..."

In Revelation 4:11, the very same state Who The Occupant is:

"You, our Lord and our God, are worthy to receive the majesty, and the honour, and the might; for You have created all things; and for Your purpose they were and are created."

He is therefore **The One *with* GOD** in the beginning, *through Whom* all things *came into existence* at the start of Creation. John then saw a book:

'...upon the right hand of the Occupant of the throne'. It was written 'inside and outside' and '...sealed down with seven seals'. Then a strong angel proclaimed '...with a loud voice', "Who is worthy to open the book, and to break its seals?" 'And no one in the heaven, or upon the earth, or under the earth, was able to open the book, nor yet to gaze upon it'.

(Revelation 5:2-5)

John 'wept much', because '...no one was found worthy to open the book, or even to gaze at it'. Then he reports, 'But one of the elders said to me':

"Do not weep, see! the Lion out of the tribe of Judah, of the root of David, has succeeded in opening the book with its seven seals."

John then saw:

"...between the throne and the four Beings, and in the *centre* of the elders, *a Lamb* placed, as having been sacrificed..."

(Revelation 5:6)

In this momentous *revelation* from **The 'Book' of Revelation**, we have a Throne upon which an Occupant sits i.e., **One Enthroned**. And **Who** was *with* **GOD** and through Whom all things were made. In close attendance are what we might perhaps term "the whole host of the heavens", Angels, Elders, and Beings. Now, however, *we also have the Lamb*, Who is able to open The Book.

Who, then, is the Lamb?

The Lamb is clearly *not* the Occupant of the Throne, for the Lamb is *between* the Throne and the four Beings. And the Occupant of the Throne is the One Who both lives for ever and ever and yet Who has created all things – "for His purpose". But He is not:

The Almighty: GOD Himself!

"For no man hath seen God at any time."

(Emphases mine.)

Once again, the answer to Who is designated as occupying the Throne lies in the earlier Scripture in this Booklet:

> "The **WORD** existed in the beginning, and the **WORD** was *with* **GOD** and the **WORD** was **GOD**.
> *He* was present *with* **GOD** at the beginning.
> **All** came into existence by means of *Him*; and nothing came into existence apart from *Him*."

The Revelation thus states the Occupant of the Throne to be the **'He'** Who was *present* with **God** 'from the beginning'. It is the same **He**, also, by Whom *everything* came into

existence and, moreover, is *The One Who Comes*.
Because this issue is so vital to a correct understanding of revelatory prophecy – *and thus to the final fate of every individual on Earth* – let us once more ask the key question of the moment:

Who is the Lamb?

Whilst the designation, Lamb, would be regarded, grammatically, as a "which" and not a "who", the sureness of the personal pronoun, He, in this case reveals that *that* description clearly refers to a person. Surely, then, the *only* logical conclusion to draw is that **the Lamb is He, Jesus.** For if we do *not* acknowledge that as the Truth here, then we have a major problem with the following passages from The Revelation:

> "And He [the Lamb] came, and **took it** [the book] **from** the right hand of the Occupant of the throne..."

(Revelation 5:7-8. Parentheses mine.)

The very word, *'from'*, is unequivocal in its **brutally-clear meaning**. Even with such clarity, however, there will yet be many who will refuse to "see"; who will refuse to acknowledge the Truth of our assertions. Paradoxically, they may well use the very book that we quote from to say it cannot be so. Indeed, they *must* use this same book, for the very many variations of Christian Church beliefs and interpretations derive their so-called *authority from* The Bible. And ultimately therefrom, also, their 'Christian mandates' which say to the faithful of all the *different, individual,* congregations: "Only *our* interpretation can be correct." Of course, all will rise or fall on exactly the interpretation clung to. So let us quote a few more Scriptural gems to further clarify the Truth of what we are saying.
Just as the host praised the Occupant on the Throne as being worthy to receive the majesty, honour and might, so do they now offer the same to the Lamb.

"Worthy is the sacrificed Lamb to receive the power, and wealth, and wisdom, and might, and honour, and majesty, and celebrity!"

(Revelation 5:12)

Both have now been *honoured equally* – as *separate Individuals!* For the next Verse very clearly illustrates this delineation between the Occupant of the Throne *and* the Lamb. The very words in Revelation 5:13-14, themselves so state it in the separative-conjunction — **"and"**!

"To the Occupant of the throne *and* to the Lamb belong the fame, the honour, the majesty, and the might for ever and ever."

A far stronger message of warning about the Truth that this Booklet contains can be read in Revelation 6:16-17. Here the same delineation, but a very firm reference to a *dual working at the end-time*, as we previously stated.

"Fall upon us, and *hide us* from the Occupant of the throne, *and from* the *displeasure* of the Lamb; for the great day of *their anger* is come – and *who is able to stand*?"

What do we understand the word, *their*, to mean? Even to the youngest English language reader it would obviously mean what it says. It means *more than one*.

This simple and short, everyday English word must surely be *the single most important pointer* to finally showing that *there are*, indeed, **Two!** – **Sons of God!** What else could possibly be needed?

If this crystal-clear Scripture is *not* proof enough for the doubters, then all that is left to finally force an awakening within their ranks will be the very *sign* of the Son of Man Himself. Just as we clearly understand the meaning of the word, *their*, I am sure we also understand the meaning of the word, *"anger"*. Associated with the previous key word, *their*, this powerful Scripture *should*, therefore, **be the one that finally awakens mankind**!

For who are **They** angry at? There can only be one group of creatures who would deserve such **Divine Wrath**. That is mankind on Earth! Who, indeed, can stand against *their* **anger**? But there is more:

> "The Salvation is from our God,
> Who sits upon the throne,
> **And from** the Lamb."

> (Revelation 7:10)

As a final entry to this key issue, Revelation 7:14-17 offers the same truth. Here, John is addressed by one of the elders who asks him if he knows who the multitude are in "white robes". John did not know so asks who they are.

> "These are they", he proceeded, "who came out of great affliction, and *they* washed *their* robes, and made them white in the blood of the Lamb. Because of *this* they are before the throne of God, and day and night they serve Him in His sanctuary; and the *Occupant of the throne* **protects them**... because the Lamb having *ascended the midst of the throne* shall **shepherd them**..."

> (Fenton. All emphases mine.)

This final reference to **The Two** from out of 'The Revelation' is interesting for more than the irrefutable Truth that there really are **Two Sons of God**. For in this particular example, we have a further clarification of very great import. Firstly, the *Occupant of the Throne* – Who therefore sits on it – *protects* the multitude who have cleansed *their* robes [*their* spirit] and made them white [pure] *themselves*. Jesus has not done it through His *acceptance* of death on the Cross. No, *they* have done it. They have achieved that state of grace by *living* His pure Teachings. And have therefore *earned the* *right* to, *metaphorically,* "stand before the Throne" and be forever protected by its Occupant.

Jesus, on the other hand, Who does not *occupy* the Throne – because He has **ascended** the **midst** of the **Throne** and therefore stands on the same level as **He** on **It** – nonetheless **shepherds** the throng. Here, also, a clear *dual* working, and one of *equal* Majesty, Power and Governance.

Notwithstanding such a clear statement about **their dual working**, we reinforce here again the especial and distinct demarcation between **The Two Sons of God**. This is defined by the fact that they possess *two different Names* – **Jesus** and **Imanuel**. And they have *two different Titles* – **Son of God** and **Son of Man**.

It is very simple to see, therefore, that they also have *two different Tasks* – for *two different Purposes*. **The Son of God**, Jesus, as The Word, also designated as **The Love of God** Who therefore works in Love, emphasised that He had '*not come to judge*'! (John 12:47)

The Son of Man as **The Will** *of* **GOD** does, however. The Will, moreover, is the *complete Will*. As we have already clearly explained, **The Son of Man** is thus **The Spirit of Truth, The Holy Spirit, The Eternal Mediator** – and thus **Justice of GOD**. It is **He** Who therefore *brings* the Judgement! Though a Judgement of **Divine Wrath**, it is a 'cleansing and sifting' nonetheless inherently imbued with the inseparable qualities of *Perfect Justice* and *Perfect Love*. And therein lies *their Dual Working*: That of **The Two Sons of God** *in the Judgement*.

Yet even though there is *individual* working contained within those designated tasks, both 'Sons' are nevertheless **in God The Father!** And **God The Father** is **in** Both! Quite simply and clearly, therefore, **"The TWO"**, and **The LORD OF ALL**, comprise:

The TRINITY! The TRIUNE GOD!

In that **Divine Reality** — the outworking and understanding of which is forever denied to we human beings — may nonetheless be understood *the meaning* of the previous Scripture from Revelation 7:10; i.e., "...our God, Who sits upon the throne..."

'The One Enthroned' is that **Part** of **The Will** of **THE TRIUNE GOD** Whom 'John the Revelator' was granted to see!

As a further reference to **A Trinity**, the prophet Zakariah (4:1-5, Fenton), in the presence of a Messenger of The Lord, describes a curious vision which the Messenger interprets for him.

> The Messenger then turned to converse with me, and roused me like a man awakened from sleep, and asked me, "What are you looking at?" When I answered, I have been looking, and saw a lamp of gold, with a cup on its top, and seven lights on its seven uprights, with seven branches for the lights, that were on its top. Two Olive trees also stood one on the right and the other on the left.
> And I continued, and asked the Messenger who was conversing with me, and said, "Tell me, Sir, what are these?" The Messenger who conversed with me accordingly replied, and asked, *"Do you not know what these are?"* And I answered, "No, Sir!"

The Messenger then explained other things to him, but Zakariah (4:11-14) insistently sought an answer to his question.

> But I continued and asked him, "What are those two Olives on the right and left of the lamps?" And I again enquired and asked him, "What are the two Olive branches that are on each side of the two golden feeders that extend from the golden standards?" And he replied to me asking, *"Do you not know what they are?"* When I answered, "No, Sir!" So he said, *"Those are the two Sons-of-oil who stand near the Master of all the earth."*

Taken all together, these explanations clearly point to a *major interpretative error* by the Christian Church and its many theologians historically. For the analyses herein really do clarify the Truth and Status of **The Trinity**. Certainly the *meaning* is clear enough; or should be for even the *basically-perceptive* reader. So the supposed *mystery* of **The Trinity** is not actually a mystery at all. Neither is it meant to be since we are enjoined by Law and **Divine Directive** to *seek* – and thus *find*!

Factually, we can certainly *know* what the *term*, Trinity, means. However, for we humans – who are merely 'developed beings' of the far lower level of **Subsequent Creation** – the 'mysterious' aspect associated with **The Divine Trinity** centres on the humanly-incomprehensible – thus *never-to-be-understood* – *concept* of: — <u>A</u>

<u>The</u> — "TRIUNE GOD"!

Human language cannot even *begin* to *express* such an 'idea', let alone somehow relate to **It** or engage with **It** meaningfully in *any* shape or form. Therefore, we must simply forever let such an *'overwhelming concept'* be the greatest **"Bible Mystery"** of all.

0.4 Destruction by "Fire"

In this Booklet we have endeavoured to use mainly **The Bible** as the key source for our revelations. We have also ventured into other areas to cull relevant and complementary knowledge to enhance our stated premise. In the closing stages of the Work it is timely to look at one especially vital aspect of **The Law**. For this *revelation* we will marry, from **The Bible**, part of **2 Peter** with part of **"The Book of Esdras"** from **The Apocrypha**.

The Books of **The Apocrypha** are not *officially* regarded as having the same degree of importance as the Books of **The Bible**. Whilst still an 'addition' or 'Addendum' to the Catholic Bible, the 'Apocryphal' Books were removed from Protestant Bibles by the British and Foreign Bible Society [primarily the Anglican Church] in the 19th century. Despite the unfortunate relegation of **The Apocrypha** to almost anonymity for probably the greater mass of global Christendom by the Church hierarchy, that body of work should nonetheless be *recognised* as being *absolutely essential* for a far greater degree of elucidation around certain key questions *in The Bible* that, at present, have no logical answers from Christendom; *as in the case of the question we address now.*

The Apocrypha, in concert *with* **The Bible**, provides the answer to it, thus giving a comprehensive picture of the whole by filling a knowledge-gap not so far addressed adequately by Christian theology. However, precisely because The Apocrypha is *officially designated* as a *lesser* work by Christendom overall, quotes from Esdras may be deemed to not carry the same authority as those from The Bible. Yet the two Books of Esdras not only provide the very answer to Peter's perhaps cryptic prophecy, but in it is *the most* **powerful** *and* **relevant** *spiritual insight and* **revelation** *for this very time* – for the Earth and **all** its peoples.

The question of "Destruction by Fire", long mulled over theologically, has now also been assessed from the scientific standpoint. From the earth-science perspective – and perhaps to a large degree from the theological side with regard to an Apocalyptic scenario – *destruction by fire* for global humanity tends towards such things as intense and widespread volcanic activity, a meteor impact, extreme drought, and perhaps prolonged solar activity.

Yet the *real answer*, whilst simple and straightforward, is ultimately *far more profound* for we human beings of Planet Earth than any notion which might suggest catastrophic events as being the *primary* driver for *destruction by fire*, and humanity *thereby* being *physically* burned. Though, of course, with certain natural phenomena, that is not just possible but very likely for some. Moreover, even for *very many* when such phenomena finally gives vent to its full power at *its* time of ordination. Now, whilst that will one day be a problematic reality for humankind, the distilled meaning of *'destruction by fire'* here means something **very, very different**.

The Book of Daniel is often used to mathematically calculate significant dates in a time-line of major events which many Christians believe reveals 'the time of the end'. Ezra, in our view clearly an important "apocalyptic prophet" in the mould of Daniel, offers a *singularly vital key* to the most crucial aspect of that approaching time; what exactly it is that will constitute the actual "force" of destruction and cleansing, and Who will bring it. Or, perhaps, **Who It was that might already have brought it!** Since we have earlier clarified the identities of both Jesus and Imanuel, the exercise we undertake now is to add considerably more weight to the outworking of **Creation-Law** for a rapidly approaching time of great upheaval.

The Prophecies of Daniel *might* have some relevance – in terms of a viable time-frame – *if* an *arrival* is still to be **expected**. However, if that has **already taken place**, in exact accordance with the many quotes already offered in this Booklet such as: "You know not the hour your Lord may come" etc., then the mathematical analyses from Daniel are logically **rendered irrelevant**. If, then, such a "return" *has occurred*, what we explain from 2 Peter and 2 Esdras equally logically fits that *possible* scenario.

Peter, towards the end of his life, offers advice to the growing numbers of Christians about what to expect at the end of the times. Fenton sub-titles Peter's discourse:

"The Irrevocable Word of God"

"You should first recognise this, that during the latter times deceivers will come with deception, gratifying their own passions, and asking, "Where is the promise of His appearing? for since the forefathers went to sleep, everything continues the same from the beginning of the creation." For they willingly suffer to hide from them this reason, that by the intention of God the skies existed from of old, and the earth with water above and water below, arranged for the purpose of God, by means of which the then existing world perished, by the water having rushed down.

But the *present earth and skies* are treasured up by His intention, '**reserved for fire**' at *a period of judgment and destruction of wicked men."*

(2 Peter:3-7, Emphases mine.)

Peter's explanation of how and why the deluge at the time of Noah was possible on the scale intimated – of which there seems to be some scientific evidence – may offer some insight into understanding the "mechanics" of it. Obviously, a lot of water had to fall to achieve an inundation sufficiently large to destroy what was on *at least part of the Earth*. Equally obviously, the water had then to drain *somewhere* for the hills to reappear. It is not our intention to delve further here, but the reader may wish to contemplate on certain passages in Genesis that "seem" to complement Peter's explanation for the "deluge". As we have previously noted, the Disciples of Jesus received far more knowledge about more aspects of the world than any other men up to that time. The key point here now is Peter's statement:

"...that the present earth and skies..." are "...**reserved for fire** *at a period of judgment and destruction of wicked men".*

The singular word **"fire"** provides the key to understanding what is not only to come, but what is *already occurring*.

What might we believe *fire* would mean in this case, however? Given that it will be a time of unimaginable desolation,

63

we could perhaps envision a huge and fiery celestial object colliding with Earth. The Revelation does state that as an actual impending event in our probable 'near-future'. Or it could perhaps be an extremely large "coronal mass ejection" (CME) from the sun which reaches out and envelopes the Earth destroying [frying] all electrical and electronic components in everything on it; from power stations to aircraft to all computerised control systems affecting every single facet of our 'modern' world. [In 2011 NASA warned that increasing solar activity would peak sharply in 2012, with the possibility of exactly that kind of damage to global electronics that did not have the necessary shielding to protect the systems from the effects of the electro-magnetic blast/s from the sun. Modern electronics are not built to withstand such power-blasts, so will "fry" should NASA's prediction be correct.]

A massive CME that blasts the *whole Earth* would therefore effectively reduce all 'first-world' countries to 'third-world' status virtually *in an instant*, for it would cause *immediate* and *irreparable* damage to the computerised control systems that regulate every facet of our lives; even food production. The fact that all power stations would be 'knocked out' means that cities would simply cease to function – for many years. The inevitable result of such a scenario would be fear and panic, and thus anarchy.

So even though the word fire usually means flames, burning and heat, does it actually mean that here? From The Apocrypha, The Book of Esdras, Chapter 13, Verse 2, the prophet Ezra recounts a dream which is afterwards interpreted for him by the "Messenger of Light". The key to understanding the meaning of the "fire" that Peter alludes to – *and would no doubt have understood* – lies in the following relevant excerpts. Initially featuring the sea wherefrom a wind arose and stirred up the waves, Ezra's dream then showed the wind make something like the figure of a man emerge from the heart of the sea. That man then:

> "...flew with the clouds of heaven...", and wherever
> he turned his face to look, "...everything under his

gaze trembled, and whenever his voice issued from his mouth...", all who heard it "...melted as wax melts when it feels the fire...".

After this Ezra beheld an "...innumerable multitude of men gathered together from the four winds of heaven..." to make war against the man who came up out of the sea. Ezra saw the "man" carve out for himself a great mountain and fly up onto it. But he was unable to see or recognise the region or place where it was. After that he saw that all who had gathered to fight him were "...much afraid, yet dared to fight". When the multitude rushed at him, "...he neither lifted his hand nor held a spear or weapon of war". But Ezra observed how he:

> "...sent forth from his mouth as it were *a stream of fire*, and from his lips *a flaming breath*, and from his tongue he shot forth *a storm of sparks*".

Ezra saw that all three were mingled together – "the stream of fire", "the flaming breath" and "the great storm". These fell on the attacking multitude and *burned them all up*. Nothing was left but the dust of ashes and the smell of smoke. After this Ezra saw the same "man" come down from the mountain and call to another multitude which was peaceable. In great fear Ezra awoke and besought an interpretation from the Most High. His petition was answered, and the key elements of the vision follow. The Messenger then spoke:

> "This is the interpretation of the vision. As for your seeing a man come up from out of the heart of the sea, *this is he whom the Most High has been keeping for many ages, who will himself deliver* **his creation**, and he will **direct those who are left**. And as for your seeing wind and fire and a storm coming out of his mouth, and as for his not holding a spear or weapon of war, yet destroying the onrushing multitude which came to destroy him, this is the interpretation."

The "interpreter" then tells Ezra that the time would come when:

"...bewilderment of mind..." would come over those "...who dwell on the earth". And they would make war against one another, "...city against city, place against place, people against people, and kingdom against kingdom". "And when these things come to pass *and the signs* **occur** *which I showed you before*, **then my Son will be revealed**, whom you saw as a man coming up from out of the sea."

The next segment from The Book of Esdras provides the link with 2 Peter. The aspects of ***primary significance*** in this particular analysis are emphasised either in italics, in bold, underlined, capitalised, or varying combinations of all.

"And when all the nations hear his voice, every man shall leave his own land and the warfare that they have against one another, and an innumerable multitude shall be gathered together, as you saw, desiring to come and conquer him - - -
And he, my Son, ***will reprove*** the assembled nations for their ***ungodliness*** [symbolised by *the storm*], and will ***reproach them to their face*** with their ***evil thoughts*** and the ***torments*** with which they are to be ***tortured*** [symbolised by *the flames*], and will ***destroy them without effort*** by ***THE LAW***." [Symbolised ***by the fire.***]

(Parenthetic additions and emphases mine.)

Here we have a clear pointer *linking* the warnings of **Peter** – thus from **The Bible** – through the clarified vision of **Ezra** – from **The Apocrypha** – to the outworking of **Creation-Law** on the affairs of mankind. Only *with* the essential contribution of the prophet, Ezra, can the *true spiritual meaning* of "**Destruction by Fire**" be answered logically. And *only* with the requisite *spiritual guidance* to *link* **The Bible** <u>*with*</u> **The Apocrypha** could we reveal that answer: An answer automatically mandated by the fact of the Perfection of **The Laws of Creation**, the explanations of which we are directed – thus graciously permitted – to offer in this and other Works of **Crystal Publishing**.

The crucial knowledge of **Creation-Law**,[6] deriving from and inherent within **Divinity Itself**, gives *back* to **The Bible** its proper place and status. The *terrible* and *inexcusable distortions* of the clear Truths in that especial Work – perversely clung to by blind millions – count strongly towards the impending *total collapse* of *all* facets of wrong *human* behaviour *and* endeavour. The associated destruction should be recognised as being produced by the *spiritually-lawful* **effect** *of the "fire"*; which is:

> "Whenever his voice issued from his mouth...", all who heard it "*...melted as wax melts when it feels the fire...*"

That is the key to understanding the effect of The Living Words of **The Law**! Whether written or spoken by **'The One'** – **The Son of Man** – Who brings 'the Complete': The **'Formed Word'** Proclaimed by **Him** is thus *transformed* into commensurate *real-time outworking* over the period of its ordained fulfilment in **The World of Matter**. And therewith is produced – under the aegis of **Inviolable Law** in Creation – the outworking of Peter's proclamatory *"destruction by fire"* upon our completely *aspiritual* global societies, cultures and religions. Quite obviously, therefore, very many of we – the *agglomerated* human race – will fully experience Peter's prophecy.[7]

Therefore, human works that comply *with* **The Law** will quite naturally prosper. Works that do not will suffer destruction. By this infallible measure we may recognise what is *true* to **The Law** and what is not. The **'fire'** of **The Law** thus unerringly produces the concomitant cleansing effect; [also **The Law**]. The powerful impact of *the storm, the*

---

[6]Fully explained in the Parent Work: BIBLE "MYSTERIES" EXPLAINED... Chapter 3: The Spiritual Laws of Creation: *The Crucial Knowledge for Humankind.* [See end of Booklet.]

[7]An 'agglomerate'; 2. a confused or jumbled mass. [Kierkegaard, Danish philosopher; "It is not the truth that lies with the masses, but the **untruth**. The **crowd** is the **untruth**."]

flames and *the fire* – which are all *already* strongly affecting mankind so detrimentally now – is solely the result of our intransigence, arrogance and stupidity in refusing to believe or accept *the one single and ultimate reality in the whole of Creation*. And that is:

That only THE LAW — <u>CREATION-LAW</u> — reigns Supreme!

There is nothing else! Everything in all of the Creations was formed from out of **The Living Law Itself: From out of The Will of GOD – IMANUEL!** It is **He** Who thus brings **The Living Law**, which is the *'cleansing fire'* spoken of in The Book of Esdras.

Therefore *what we even now experience* is nevertheless still just the beginnings of the storm, the flames and the fire – **The Law.** Is His arrival imminent? Or is He already here? Difficult questions for most, but crucial for all! The appearance of the Sign of The Son of Man "in the sky" is the key to the fulfilment of the last events for an intransigent humanity. Since His Sign "appears in the sky", we can expect that it will be a powerful one. One, therefore, that cannot be missed, even by the obtuse.

Though what will it *actually* herald? That He is about to "descend on clouds", that He is about to be born, or perhaps to be revealed? Or perhaps it will state that He really *did* "...come like a thief in the night...", that only *the few* were awake, and that the world had therefore *missed The Event*.

Because His Sign is connected with Him, it will be visible to all human spirits in this part of "the world" and not just to those living on Earth at the time. Therefore, both the living and the physically dead will know that the Sign, **clearly visible to all then**, is here!

0.5　The 'Rapture'? A Distortion of Bible Truth!

The expected return of Jesus by one very large, mainly American, group of Christians involves, for them, the interesting notion that they, and they alone as a group from all humankind, will be "saved" by being "raptured". The concept of "The Rapture" as applied in this case takes the form of an event or process more fully formulated from earlier ideas mooted by an evangelical preacher, John Nelson Darby, who arrived in the U.S. in 1862. His minister, Cyrus Scofield, expanded the evangelist's ideas in the prominent Scofield Reference Bible.

Drawn from the Apostle Paul's seeming assertion that believers could or would be "lifted up to Christ in heaven", the idea of being "raptured to heaven" must presuppose that it is in the physical body since it all happens in an instant. That at least seems to be the general conviction of believers. However, we have already correctly concluded that according to The Almighty's Perfect and thus Unchangeable Laws – which accord with Perfect, natural, Laws derived from the higher Spiritual paradigm – *human physical bodies cannot be suddenly transformed and/or whisked away to sit on clouds or something similar.*

Even The Son of God Himself could not circumvent The Perfect Laws that He came to fulfil: "I come not to overthrow the Laws..." Flesh and blood bodies do not float. They are not "lighter than air" vehicles.

"So what really did happen to the body of Jesus?"

You, the reader, can **now know** where His body actually lies. It is secured in *a special tomb under Jerusalem*. It is a crucified body, **but without the legs broken.**

Here, in revelatory clarification from the Parent Work, **BIBLE "MYSTERIES" EXPLAINED**...: The body that served The Son Of God on Earth rests in a sealed cavern under Jerusalem. At the entrance to the cave three crosses are engraved over the right hand arch. The body inside will show evidence of crucifixion, **but the bones in the legs** are <u>not</u> **broken.** In the row of upper teeth in the skull, *an eye-tooth is missing.* And on the gravestone which covers His body is engraved a specific mark or sign: **His Sign!**

The missing eye-tooth or canine is obviously singularly significant. But why have we emphasised the fact that the legs on this especial body are not broken?

We will once more note the prophecy about that key pointer:

> "The soldiers, therefore, came and broke the legs of the first, as well as of the other one crucified with Him; but when they came to Jesus, and seeing that He was already dead, *they did not break His legs.* And the eye-witness gives this evidence, and his evidence is truthful; and he himself knows that he speaks true, so that you may believe. For these events happened in order that the Scripture might be verified: *A BONE OF HIM SHALL NOT BE BROKEN.*"
>
> (John 19:32-37, Fenton's Capitalisation. Emphases mine.)

Do Christians really believe that the **non-material** and therefore **Eternal 'Realm'** of what is so loosely designated as 'heaven' is some kind of jaunt *'just up there'*? Jesus told Pilate that His Kingdom was *not* of *this* world. And to His Disciples that He would *return to* The Father and they would see Him *'no more'*. How can it be that many millions will accept an idea that is an absolute impossibility according to the Perfect Laws of He Whose teachings of Perfect Truth those same millions *profess* to believe in and follow?

Phenomenal sales of the "Left Behind" series which promote the "rapture" concept and which have apparently sold somewhere around 50 million copies, clearly point to at least that many believers. Yet the sage observation of key Scriptures of warning should be made by all who wish to be "raptured":

"I tell you indeed that you shall not depart until all has been fulfilled," – "Not one farthing shall be remitted you until *you* have paid fully."

And for the authors who have made millions of dollars but in the process of growing rich *already led millions astray now*:

"What does it profit a man if he gains the whole world and loses his soul?"

Should we designate the so-called "rapture" to be some kind of "Bible mystery"? After all, men prefer a mystery to Truth! No, it is not any kind of "Bible mystery" simply because the concept of "rapture", *as taught and believed by people in the Christian Church,* **is completely wrong**.

It is more an emotive concept ultimately derived from indulging human religious weaknesses. It does not exist and will not happen because the whole idea actually *opposes* all notions of necessarily **Perfect Laws** deriving from **GOD**. Disbelieving or dismissive Christians at this time of rapidly approaching "closures" will one day soon reel in shock and horror as the cold truth of these statements becomes brutally clear.

The rapid approach of the *end* of human foolishness, driven by increasing pressure from **The Light** Above, therefore means that all human concepts are exposed to the **Power** of that relentless *pressure*. In the case of the notion of 'The Rapture', its time of exposure and belief is perhaps at, or nearing, its peak. It has therefore gone through the necessary phase of revealing itself in its true nature; it has offered itself as a concept to those who have chosen it as truth; those choices have thus largely been made; and all that is left now is *its collapse at the appointed time,* **and therewith its demise**. There is therefore no further need to comment on what will almost certainly be:

The greatest non-event in human history!

71

0.6   THE PROCLAMATION!

The terribly wrong teaching of 'The Rapture' by the Christian Church pales into *insignificance* when compared with the *greatest distortion* of all; that there has only ever been *one* Son of GOD. The powerful outworking of **The Law** from ordained scriptural prophecy is perfectly proclaimed here in the Divine Warning:

"Vengeance [THE LAW] is mine, I will repay."

The Law will thus visit its terrifying reciprocity on *all* who subscribe to this *appalling distortion* of **The Living Truth!**

Everyone wants from their God a soft, enervating, vacillating, personalised, emotionally-satisfying, earthly brand of constant and all-forgiving love. Few there are who *really understand* that **Justice** is an *absolute* accompaniment of **The Love** of **The Divine!** Distorting the Truth from Above sets all who so distort it *against* that very Truth, and thus *against* its **Source:**

THE ALMIGHTY!

The knowledge about The Two Sons of GOD is, therefore, *the most "Crucial Imperative" of all* – for *all* humankind. This key Truth is not about being some kind of 'Christian truth', nor is it a point to be debated by so-called 'experts'. The religious scholars and leaders of *all* ethnic groups and cultures and *all* religions, no matter how derived, must face this Truth here, *now*, at this critical juncture in human history and evolution.

That evolution was never about the "human/chimp" split that occurred millions of years ago; that scientists have placed so much importance on. We have clearly refuted the totally incorrect *scientific obsession* surrounding that foolish belief in a Sister Booklet: 'Whither Cometh Humankind: The Origins of Man, Genesis and Science Agree'; and in Chapter 2 of Parent Work. [See end of Booklet.] So much wasted time and energy and research funding that would have been better spent examining subjects that could *really* benefit man.

The crucial recognition that we are not just a physical body solely is thus the key to understanding that the Earth is a place of "physical transition" only, and that our *actual* evolution was always meant to have been that of our *spiritual selves*, the *true* human being. However, just as primatologists, anthropologists and many other "...ologists" etc., have wasted valuable "spiritual-life" time pursuing something that was totally irrelevant for *real* human knowledge so, too, have the many "Christian scholars" also wasted the same kind of valuable "life-resource" in promoting completely wrong interpretations about what is the ultimate "Truth" given to mankind in The Bible:

The "Living Truth" of The <u>Two</u> Sons of GOD.

Religious scholars and ethnic and cultural leaders of belief-systems that ignore, disbelieve or outright oppose or condemn this Ultimate Truth will – **along with Christian Church leaders who also disbelieve or deny and thus lead astray** – live the full experience of the outworking of one of the very Laws that **One** of The Two Sons of GOD stated unequivocally He had "...not come to *overthrow*, but to fulfil."

Earth-science and all the great religions state that key Law in basically similar terms; *'The Law of Sowing and Reaping', 'The Iron Law of Karma'* – **'The Law of Reciprocal Action'**. We can quite rightly therefore say that *no* reasons or excuses exist anywhere in the total human science/religious paradigm whereby the outworking of that great Law – with regard to the Truth *about* **The Two Sons of GOD** – could **not** be recognised. Do we not see the effect of the increasing power of this Inviolable Law every day now?

The recognition of **The Two Sons** [i.e., **Parts or Extensions of GOD**] therefore represents the critical, spiritual evolutionary-step on the path to what is meant to be humankind's final goal – *our return home*. The recognition of this sublime Truth is thus also meant to be the same kind of evolutionary step that all leaders and teachers of all religious beliefs world-wide must make, **so that The Pure Truth of He Who gave us Life could be gifted to all.** The explanations in this Work will help lead the *serious* reader to that complete knowledge.

Throughout this Booklet we have alluded to the "possibility" that **The One Who Comes** *has already been*. Since He is to be expected at a time of great travail for the human race, we have striven to pique the curiosity and spiritual intuition of you, the reader, to seriously consider what we have stated here.

Because a statement about such an event would necessarily have to be proclamatory in nature, an absolute proclamation centred around **His Return** would therefore not be at all subject to intellectual analyses – *for such analyses would automatically be rendered irrelevant* **by The Event Itself!**

At the conclusion of this key Booklet, therefore, we unequivocally proclaim what is perhaps – for the Christian Church particularly, but mankind collectively – the greatest "truthful irony" of all:

Bible prophecy has been fulfilled, and "the world" has missed The Event!

Thus for all: – Bible Scholars, Popes, Archbishops, Presidents and Kings; politicians of *every* persuasion, scientists and writers, leaders of *all* Religions and Churches and of *all* ethnic and cultural Groups:

The *"Dual Working"* has therefore been fulfilled, and thus the key confirmatory-proclamation by **Jesus** that:

74

"He, Himself, will Honour Me!"

*   *   *   *   *

JESUS — The SON OF GOD —

– is thus **Honoured** in the **All-TRUTH** brought to
Earth by:

IMANUEL — The SON OF MAN

— The ETERNAL MEDIATOR —

['GOD with us!']

*   *   *   *   *

In the profound Grace of this knowledge, and in accordance
with the Mandate to so proclaim, we herewith present our
Proclamation:

**The SON OF MAN has indeed come like a thief in
the night and He has gifted to humankind HIS
"Message" — His ALL-TRUTH!**

More decisively, however, we offer here:

HIS Admonition:

"You Can See It – If You Are Willing To See!"

Bibliography

1. The deeper knowledge in this Booklet is derived from the Work: **IN THE LIGHT OF TRUTH**; **The Grail Message** by **Abd-ru-shin**. Stiftung Gralsbotschaft Publishing Co., Stuttgart, Germany.

2. *The Holy Bible in Modern English*, Ferrar Fenton, Destiny Publishers, Massachusetts U.S.A. 1966 Edition.

3. *The Holy Bible, Authorised (King James) Version*, Eyre and Spottiswoode (Publishers) Ltd., Great Britain.

4. *The Jerusalem Bible, Reader's Edition 1985*, First published 1968, Darton, Longman and Todd Ltd., London.

5. *New American Standard Bible*, Text Edition. Thomas Nelson Publishers. Copyright: The Lockman Foundation. Printed in the USA.

6. *The Apocrypha of the Old Testament*, Revised Standard Version, Published by Thomas Nelson and Sons Ltd.

7. *BIBLE "MYSTERIES" EXPLAINED: Understanding "Global Societal Collapse" from The "Science" in The Bible: What Every Scientist, Bible Scholar and Ordinary Man Needs to Know.* Charles S. Brown [Copyright 2007 and 2009] First published in 2007 by Crystal Publishing, New Zealand.

8. *The History Channel* The Documentary Series: "How Life Began". Screened 2009.

9. *The National Geographic Channel* Documentaries: "Birth of Life" and "Human Ape". Screened 2009.

0.7   The Parent Book:

Formerly:

"The Gathering Apocalypse and World Judgement;
What It Brings – Even Now – And Why"

Available in **New Zealand** at:
http://www.publishme.co.nz

Or at www.crystalbooks.org

Now:

BIBLE "MYSTERIES" EXPLAINED
[Revised Second Edition]
Understanding "Global Societal Collapse" from The "Science" in The Bible;
What Every Scientist, Bible Scholar and Ordinary Man Needs to Know!

> The **Revised Second Edition** of this book is more comprehensive in that it now explains How and Why the 2008 global economic collapse occurred, but also when the seeds that wrought the How and Why were sown, and by whom. [Chapter 3. **The Spiritual Laws: The Necessary Knowledge**
> 3.3.3 The Interlinked Global Monetary System "Reaping The Whirlwind." A Brief History Lesson.]

> Additional information about the events surrounding the last day of Jesus's life, from His arrest in the Garden of Gethsemane to His murder at Golgotha, is now included.
> The interesting question of the "Seven Churches in Asia-Minor" from The Book Of Revelation is

examined more critically. Necessarily using the discoveries and mathematics of present-day astronomy/cosmology, the revealing conclusion of the true meaning perfectly resonates with the intuitive perception of the great mathematician, astronomer, theologian and scientist, Sir Isaac Newton.

This book, the result of many years of inner seeking and empirical research, offers *serious* seekers of the Truth a comprehensive understanding of the origin, meaning and purpose of human life; material and spiritual.

Beginning with **The Crucial Imperatives: Nine key points** that *must* be taken into consideration if logical and reasoned answers to humankind's Whence, Whither and Why is *ever* to be understood; the book takes the reader step by step through an understanding of man's **Spiritual Origins, The Spiritual Laws of Creation**, the difference between **The First Death** and **The Second Death; Elemental Lore** [of Nature]; **Jesus! His Birth, Death and Resurrection** [a revisionist analysis]; before examining the truly 'mind-expanding' meaning of **"The 7 Churches in Asia"** from **The Book of Revelation**.

The key knowledge helps explain *why* there actually are **Two Sons of God**– final Chapter. It is key precisely because all other knowledge stems from that reality.

On reading the Work, the genuine seeker will clearly see that a conditioning process, set in place by religious authorities from the outset, over millennia has wrought appalling suffering through their inexcusable distortions of the Teachings of **The Truth** that once issued pristine and sublime from the Pure Holiness of its Bringer: **Jesus, The Son Of God!**

Now, because of those distortions, humankind is as a rudderless wreck on an increasingly stormy sea. Our many and increasing problems were not brought upon us by any kind of arbitrary randomness, but through *our constant and stubborn refusal to live according to the very Laws of Life which **alone** guarantee knowledge, peace and harmony.*

At the same time, however, – and precisely through the knowledge of those Laws – the way is shown in *how* we can *change* global societies *for the better.* Quite logically, if we continue down our present path for much longer *without such change*, the immutable outworking of **The Law** *will simply bring to an end* all that which *human thought and endeavour* had sought to establish and/or erect *in place of* the immutable and inviolable aegis of: **The One Law!** — — —

CREATION-LAW!

The Parent Work explains the How, the What and the Why!

Available in N.Z. at:
http://www.publishme.co.nz

Or – **http://www.crystalbooks.org**

Table of Contents

4 Elemental Lore Of Nature

5 JESUS: His Birth, Death and Resurrection

6 Stigmata

7 Right Bible/Wrong Bible

8 The Emergence of Language

9 The First Death

THE BOOKLET SERIES

*   *   *   *   *

THE TWO SONS OF GOD

The Son of Man and The Son of God
What The Bible Really Says

*   *   *   *   *

JESUS!:
His Birth, Death and
Resurrection

A Revisionist Analysis of the "Sacrosanct"
Christian Viewpoint

*   *   *   *   *

THE SPIRITUAL LAWS OF CREATION

The Crucial Knowledge for Humankind

*   *   *   *   *

WHITHER COMETH HUMANKIND?

(The Origins of Man) *Genesis and Science Agree*

*   *   *   *   *

THE "7 CHURCHES" Of THE
"REVELATION"

What the "Hubble" Will Never See
Sir Isaac Newton's "Plan of The World"

*   *   *   *   *

www.ingramcontent.com/pod-product-compliance
Lightning Source LLC
Chambersburg PA
CBHW071833020426
42331CB00007B/1715